John Lindsay

Practice in Cotton-Carding
A complete manual for the card room of the cotton mill

ISBN/EAN: 9783337271909

Printed in Europe, USA, Canada, Australia, Japan

Cover: Foto ©Andreas Hilbeck / pixelio.de

More available books at **www.hansebooks.com**

PRACTICE

IN

COTTON-CARDING.

A Complete Manual for the Card
Room of the Cotton Mill.

With full detailed instructions respecting the operation and manipulation of Cotton-cards, with
instructions respecting the surmounting
of special difficulties and with all
necessary calculations.

By JOHN LINDSAY,

Carding-Master.

Published by
THE TEXTILE RECORD,
425 Walnut Street, Philadelphia.
1888.

Price 75 Cents.

UNIFORM WITH THIS BOOK.

Textile Record Hand-book No. 1, Practice in Wool Carding, by Joseph Brown, Price, 50 cents.
Textile Record Hand-book No. 2, Practice in Finishing Woolens and Worsteds, by F. H. Greene, Price, 50 cents.
Textile Record Hand-book No. 3, Practice in Weaving and Loom Fixing, by B. D. Nightingale, Price, 75 cents.

THE TEXTILE RECORD

is a first class monthly textile magazine, devoted wholly to the textile manufacturing industry in all its branches.

The TEXTILE RECORD contains in each number more original matter than any other textile journal in the world.

The contents of this hand-book indicate the character of the material in THE TEXTILE RECORD. Its contributors include the most expert practical workers in America and Europe.

THE TEXTILE RECORD in each number is richly illustrated.

Subscription price, $3.00 a year.

OPINIONS.

Fairmount Worsted Mills, Phila., "We consider the Textile Record one of the most valuable textile papers now published." Conshohocken, (Pa.) Worsted Mills, "We think here that your paper is invaluable." Beargrass Woolen Mills, Louisville, Ky., "The Textile Record never fails to make the rounds of our mill." Miami Woolen Mills, Hamilton, Ohio, "The Textile Record is in our opinion, one of the foremost papers devoted to the textile interests." Knowles Woolen Mills, New Castle, Del., "It is the best textile paper I have ever seen." Rockwell's Woolen Mills, Tiffin, Ohio, "Permit us to express our high regard for the Textile Record." Grafton Worsted Mills, Milwaukee, Wis., "We are greatly pleased with the Textile Record." Dunham Hoisery Co., Naugatuck, Conn., "A very useful and interesting publication." St. Paul, (Minn.), Knitting Works, "The best journal of the kind published." South Union Mill, Rockingham, N. C. "We like the Textile Record very much." Stony Creek Mills, Reading, Pa., "We like your journal very much." Turner's Falls (Mass.), Cotton Mills, "One of the ablest, clearest spoken and most reliable of papers." Southern Woolen Mfg. Co., Louisville, Ky., "Very complete in its several departments." Chester Woolen Mills, Coatesville, Pa., "One of the best mediums for conveying the advanced ideas of American textile manufacturers." Rosalie Mills, Natchez, Miss., "One of the best, if not the best, periodicals we have, bearing on mill subjects." Wallingford Mills, Del. Co., Pa., "It has uniformly given us satisfaction." Lowell (Mass.) Hosiery Co., "A useful and valuable paper for any mill manager."

Price, $3.00 a year.

TABLE OF CONTENTS.

CHAPTER VII.

CARDING FOR COMBED YARNS.

Page

CHAPTER VIII.

COMBING THE COTTON FIBRE.

CHAPTER IX.

DOUBLING AND DRAWING THE SLIVER.

CHAPTER X.

DRAWING AND TWISTING.

CHAPTER XI.

DIFFICULTIES PRACTICALLY OVERCOME.

CHAPTER XII.

CARD ROOM CALCULATIONS.

CHAPTER I.

PRELIMINARY.

SELECTING THE STOCK—MIXING—SOME PRACTICAL SUGGES-
TIONS—DOUBLING ON THE LAPPER—OPENING THE COTTON
—NOTES ON THE PREPARATION OF THE FIBRE.

Selecting the Stock.—In dealing with the
difficulties to be met with in picking and carding
cotton, we must not let the selection of the stock
and the bearing it has on the strength and uniformity of the thread pass unheeded. No matter
how well the preparing department may be attended to, ill-sorted cotton cannot be spun into
even, fair yarn. Coarse, harsh fibres and those
of the silky kind will not pick or card together.
They will not draw or twist together, any better
than will fibres of different lengths. Both lead to
bad work, which can only be avoided by proper
classification. In this business good judgment is
gained only by close study of the structure, size,
and general formation of the fibres. The precise
adaptation of the cotton to the mixing, and therefore to the practical working, becomes a positive
necessity in all manufacturing establishments
which work upon progressive principles. .Hence
comparisons made with regard to the spirality,

5

oily matter and general characteristics of the staple are very uncertain without microscopic aid. Yet in the hands of an expert sampler, the mature fibre may be detected from the immature, and a mixing prepared from which the largest amount of profit can be obtained.

Mixing the Stock.—The indications of matured cotton, which can be discerned without mechanical assistance, are creaminess of color, spirality of structure, evenness and conformity, and consistency and strength. It is always understood that the mixing must be suitable to the requirements of the counts, and the cotton and waste so graded that the goods will be regular and saleable. Hence the inferior staple and the waste must receive special attention, so that too great a proportion of either may not be sorted together, and the strength and elasticity of the thread thereby at any time impaired.

The fly, strip and roving waste, as well as that picked from the more advanced processes, should be run through the opener and made into laps so that it can be spread on the mixing with greater regularity. The low bales must also receive due attention, and have their proper courses on the mixing, and the cotton must be drawn from a perpendicular face. The management of mixings has a decided effect on the general producing powers of the machinery.

Because in this country we use a better quality of stock for the same number than is used elsewhere, that should be no reason why there should not be as much thoroughness as possible employed in the handling of it, and every practical means taken to insure good work.

Superior preparation means the smallest possible quantity of waste. It keeps the production to the maximum by sending all the fibres forward, and takes care that little is returned to be paid for over again. Besides, waste invariably weakens the yarn, and it also generates nits.

Experience has taught that the custom of opening the bales some time before mixing gives the fibre a chance to absorb moisture and to recover its natural body. When the stock is allowed to release itself in this manner, it works better, there is less waste returned, and it removes the conditions which cause sticky laps. A moderate degree of moisture in the air is very necessary where the mixing stands. This is an object of importance, inasmuch as it permits less electricity in the preparing and the shell, leaf, seed and sand are much more easily separated.

On account of the varying circumstances in actual practice, it is impossible to offer here any rules to be strictly followed in mixing. Our intention is merely to throw such light as has been developed by experience on the system of

classifying the cotton to fit the requirements of the different counts, leaving it to the judgment of the practical manager if there is any room for improvement in his present methods, or whether there is such attention paid to the mixing of the stock as will prevent irregular spinning.

Opening.—The work required from the opener is such as to necessitate a considerable degree of care. This machine takes the place of the willow, now almost obsolete, and contends with the material in its rude state. The lumps fed on must not be very bulky, else the rollers cannot compress them without rising out of gear and breaking the continuity of the lap, thus causing such confusion as often results in breakages and lengthy stops. The sand is very troublesome here, and is likely to choke the channels of egress prepared for it. If these are not cleaned often and well, the duties assigned to this machine will be left to others in which the facilities for purifying are not sufficient, and the seeds and motes are therefore carried forward. The burden devolving on the cards is materially lightened when the machines which open the fibre and egest the seeds and foreign matter are intelligently handled.

An opener (unless there be a preparer attached) ought to have but one beater. In this instance the labor-saving idea has proceeded too far, to

the detriment of the quality of the production. This is the place above all others in which there is ample accommodation, as well as opportunity, to mix and remix the stock, and to make certain preparation for round, regular and uniformly strong thread. This can be accomplished by having machines with fewer beaters and more lattice tables for doubling, a thing which machines with numerous beaters do not accomplish.

Doubling on the Lapper.—The most practical method of assimulating the fibres is found to be by doubling on the lappers. The advantages to be gained from this are much more appreciated in practice in England than with us, and this is one of the reasons why very poor cotton is used for coarse counts there. Good work one day and bad the next, from the same mixing, warns us that we are not putting sufficient doublings on the lapper to prevent the stock from being alternately weak and strong. The carding-engines may be in the best order and yet if the material is not sufficiently doubled in the picker-room some bad spinning cannot be avoided.

There are other occurrences with this machine which if permitted, will cause variations in the work. The grids and screes over which the cotton passes should at all times be free from any accumulation of sand or bunches of fibre. These impede the flight of the cotton over the grids,

and alter the direction so as to make heavy-sided laps, and to cause poor carding where the bulk is fed in. The screw cylinders must be kept clear of bunches, to allow the draught of the fans to act uniformly and to remove the short and dead fibre. The beaters should be gauged so that the seeds which fall under will equal in quantity the full width of the feed. If not, these seeds are passing through and will be seen sticking in the doffers of the cards. Dirty grids, foul screes, and choked fan-ways, will prevent the short from being taken out at the proper place, and the result will be dirty carding.

CHAPTER II.

.

CARDING COTTON.

GENERAL REFLECTIONS ON THE SUBJECT—SINGLE CARDING
—NECESSARY CONDITIONS FOR DOING IT WELL—DOUBLE
CARDING AND ITS ADVANTAGES—CARD CLOTHING AND
ITS PROPER APPLICATION.

The end to be aimed at.—The importance
attached to the manner in which the cotton is
treated on the cards, is shown by the efforts con-
stantly made to produce engines of greater capacity and perfection of work. Practical spinners
agree that a good, round, clean thread cannot be
manufactured unless the carding is uniform in
staple and excellent in quality. To attain this
end is the aim of every intelligent and enterpris-
ing carder. Valuable assistance has been rendered by developments in the other machinery,
but still it remains for the well-ground and well-
set card to clear the material, separate the fibres
and make the process of good spinning easy.

The carder of to-day has many advantages
over his predecessors and is therefore expected
to produce better results. His cards, his clothing,
and his apparatus for grinding, are all so much

superior in every respect to those of twenty years ago that, with ordinary precaution and intelligence, he cannot fail to obtain a better result from a similar grade of cotton. Still, good engines may be set up and well started, but through bad management they may, in a short time, be doing irregular and unsatisfactory work. On the other hand the false economy of working the clothing too long may be the source of much mischief in that direction. Hence, if we desire to know when a thing is wrong, the cause of it going wrong, and the best and most expeditious means to put it right, we must have expert men in charge of the carding.

Points in Good Carding.—To deliver a sliver thoroughly clean and perfectly straightened, the wire points on the cylinder, the top flats and the doffer should be quite adequate to comb and separate every fibre. The cotton ought to be handled with skill and intelligence, and given to the engines in such a manner as certainly to insure the above results. This degree of perfection can be attained only by light carding. On single carding from 45 to 55 grains to the yard of sliver has been decided by experience to be a good standard for common top—flat heads. Machines of greater capacity ought to be taxed only in proportion. Good single carding requires to have well-selected stock,

clean, ripe and of a uniform length. By carding single with a draft of from 50 or 55 to one, with the above-mentioned stock, excellent results will be attained for counts from 36s down.

Over-Carding and Over-Drafting. — It must be remembered that single carding may be over-done; that is to say, the fibres may be carded too much while in one position. Most of the straightening and combing properties of a carding engine are between the feed rolls and the cylinder, and on single carding it is evident the staple is combed but one way; that is, over one end, while the other is being held by the feed rolls. If this end is held too long, the result is over-carding at one end, enfeebling this part of the fibre, and leaving it unfit to be drawn out properly, or in a condition to unite closely.

This is the outcome of over-drafting, because the greater the draft the slower revolve the feed rolls, and therefore the more carding the ends of the fibre next to the cylinder receive. Hence the fibres are left to pass on, with (so to speak) thick, stubby ends, and the other processes are unable to unite them in anything like the glossy condition which it is their natural tendency to assume. Increasing the velocity of the cylinder has the same effect, and adds to the waste through centrifugal force. Lickers-in remedy this to some extent by partially combing one end

of the fibre and delivering the other end to the cylinder. Lickers-in are effective in this manner on single engines of large capacity, where soft, short and clean cotton is used, and great product is expected. Still, the process of straightening and separating the fibre is not so complete as when carded double without lickers-in. Hence the necessity for well-selected stock for single carding.

The Top-flat Card.—Attention is strongly directed just now to the top-flat card which is coming into general use. When operated double it makes the best kind of work. It combs, straightens, and softens the fibres, and removes the impurities more perfectly than any other. These qualities are very desirable for fine "counts." On medium as well as fine yarns, this card is also much liked, and even where coarse numbers are required to be soft and even, it is likely to be in the first rank. Extensive improvements in almost every part of this engine have been made from time to time. Still if we except the stripping attachment, it does not differ greatly from the engines of Greaves, Peel, Burly, Marsden and Murray of two centuries ago. From a foot and a half it has been gradually increased to double that width, which is the recognized standard.

Double-Carding.—Very good single card-

ing, certainly, we have seen made for counts as high as 40s, while on the other hand, we have seen double-carded stock for the same numbers, which was no more than fair. The reason for this may not always be found in the machine, or in its method of construction. It is in the picking machinery, or in the selecting of the cotton, that the trouble is most likely to be found. The drafts, speeds and quantity produced may account in some degree for the inferiority of the work, and although these are in the line of the skilled overseer, cannot, under the circumstances, be touched. Indeed, it often happens, that the quantity demanded per inch of carding surface hinders to a great extent, the overseer in the application of his skill; the qualities commonly desired in such a man being those of the pushing kind. The small black nit, the broken, prongy seed and leaf, which cannot be removed by the lapper beaters and which are to be met with at all points and are so obnoxious when exposed in the cloth and yarn, cannot be taken out unless the fibre is double carded or combed; that is, reversed and operated on in both directions. When carding double the drafts are always light, and so arranged that no damage can be done to the staple, either in the first or second process. The doublings gained, but which are entirely lost in single carding, are invaluable in moving

and assimilating the fibre. The large extra doubling of fibres, with the two combing processes bringing to stock such a fine state of separation, cannot possibly be equaled by single carding, however slow or lightly delivered.

The effect of carding double is to make the yarn and goods smooth and glossy, to give them just such qualities as are desirable and profitable. By changing the position of fibres they are really strengthened, because the dirt is more thoroughly taken out, and the straightening action is made more complete. The double combing by the card wire gives gloss to the yarn and the freedom from dirt gives strength; for in such condition the fibres lie more closely and ·evenly together.

Clothing the Cards.—We will next consider the clothing of the cylinders, a kind of work which is not done on the card every year and therefore ought to be executed with neatness, and at the same time, with a view to permanency. A job of this sort is not executed for show, but a neat and a strong job is easy in the hands of a good workman.

In the first place, strike a line around the cylinder for each end of the sheets. Be sure that every sheet touches this line, and nothing over. These lines can be best drawn by turning the cylinder against a pencil held steadily on the

string-piece. Parallel lines, by which to square the sheets, are made perfectly exact, by having the the straight-edge fixed firmly on the segments in which the top-flat-pins are screwed, and by moving the cylinder the required distance for each line. From centre to centre of the plugs (or the distance the tacks must be apart) should be marked on a nice piece of wood no longer than the cylinder. Stick tacks according to these marks, and good, regular, workmanlike tacking-on will be made sure. Be careful to lay the sheet square on the line marked out for it, and at the extreme ends drive a tack part way, then one in the middle, and another in the quarter distance. When the sheet is in this position take another look to make sure that it stands square on the lines. If so, stick and drive the tacks carefully until the one side of the sheet is nailed on.

Stretching and Backing..—We now come to the most important part of the work, the stretching and backing. It may be stated here that a machine for clothing cards should be strong and rigid, the teeth in the ratchet small in pitch, well tempered and sharp, so that there will be no "give" or let back to the stretch. The same precaution is necessary with the dog by which the cylinder is bound. Heavy paper cut the exact size of the sheet, and pasted so that it cannot move with the pull, is generally used for

backing. Now draw the end of the sheet square
with the margin line, and tack to the same line
at the other end. Each time the pliers are shifted
great care must be taken that the ratchet is
moved the same distance, else the sheet will be
pulled laterally, which will cause trouble at the
finish by trimming the part drawn over the line.
The judgment of the practical operator is the
best rule that can be given for stretching the
sheets. Leather is not always alike, some parts
on the same sheet will stretch more than others.

In clothing the doffer, the margin at each end
must not project beyond that of the cylinder. A
good way is to divide the circumference of the
doffer in as many equal spaces as there are rows
of teeth in the fillet. Split these rows and tack
tightly and carefully. During the winding-on be
sure, whether it is done with a machine or by
hand, to have the same tension all the time.

The Usage of Card Clothing.—An intelligent conception of what is required of the card
clothing tends to preserve it and to keep the carding good and uniform. Vulcanized rubber-faced
clothing is one of the best substitutes for all
purposes for which leather is used, and is
rapidly superceding it. When leather hardens
on account of exposure to water and oil, as in
wool carding, this clothing runs without injury.
It has also a valuable feature in the firm and

elastic support it furnishes to the teeth. In clothing with this foundation the holes contract about the wire more closely than on leather, thus securing an important factor towards durability. Before putting on, it should be conditioned somewhat like the natural rubber-faced clothing, by keeping it for several days and nights in a temperature a few degrees higher than where it is to run. If this is attended to the cloth will, on account of the decrease of temperature, slightly tighten up after it is nailed on. Cylinders on which natural rubber-clothing is used should be free from paint, or any under-pinning in which there is oil. Cotton cloth put on with some harmless paste, such as is made from flour, and given time to dry, has been known to give good satisfaction. Day and night the temperature in the room where rubber clothing is used must be kept the same. When exposed to a low temperature the teeth become so hard that the carding is spoiled, while loose clothing and fillets are found to be caused by a rise in the temperature.

CHAPTER III.

GRINDING THE CARDS.

PREPARING A CARD FOR THE GRINDER—THE BEST KINDS OF GRINDERS—COVERING GRINDERS—IMPORTANT HINTS AND SUGGESTIONS—PUTTING THE GRINDER ON THE CARD—CONSIDERATIONS TO BE CAREFULLY OBSERVED—POINTS ABOUT GOOD GRINDING—THE CARE OF TOP-FLATS—CARD SETTING.

The man who does the grinding.—The trustworthiness of the man who is to do the grinding of a card may be estimated from the way in which, after stripping the cylinder, he looks over and studies the card. His purpose should be to find out how the wire, cloth and fillets have stood the strain and the wear and tear during the interval which has elapsed since the last grinding and setting were done. Much information may be gained here, which is difficult and troublesome to get at on any other occasion. The engine with mountings and covers removed, stripped clean and brushed free from fibre, after having run its full quota of time, which may be three, four, or even five weeks, offers a good opportunity to a practical man to ascertain what the card is doing and what it is likely to continue

to do. It also gives him a chance to determine whether anything is necessary to be done to it before grinding again. A few minutes spent on each card at this time will be found profitable, and if the ascertained information be put into practice, will tend to maintain its condition.

If the cylinder and doffer are both rubbed at the same place it shows that the doffer has been running too close. A rubbed cylinder and a sharp doffer, point to the licker-in or feed rolls ; the one or the other as the case may be. A licker-in rubbed blunt, indicates the feed rolls ; and if glazed but sharp, the cylinder. Loose top-flat sheets will rub only the cylinder and are always discovered when running the "flats." A tack out of the top-flat, will rub a narrow ring around the cylinder, while the same thing will happen to the "doffer" when there is a tack out on the cylinder cloth. Loose clothing will rub doffer and flats alike. All of these must be looked to, and remedied before the card is started up again.

If the licker-in is doing its duty, it ought to be free from strip, and the hard tempered wire teeth in good condition. If not, it is ready for the grinder, because it is either rubbed or hooked, and in no condition suitable for egesting filth. This is of considerable importance when carding with lickers-in ; so much so, that it is often found to be necessary when at work, to lift the cover

and see if the topside is clean. If it is not, it is dropping good fibre, and producing nitty carding.

The fillets.—Much harm may follow from not giving special attention to the fillets at this time. These always tighten, with the heft of grinding, at the end where the winding·on begins, and frequently tear or break. All fillets ought to be looked over and made secure before grinding. They should be drawn up neatly, and all the ragged teeth removed from the edges. Before the card is ready for the grinder, the wire must be drawn up with the card knife in good shape and all the jammed wire picked up, and tubed into line. Each sheet of clothing must be gone over in this way, and care taken to find out if any slack or blistered parts have escaped notice. If the picking up of the fallen teeth is neglected, for any length of time, the standing wires will get ground so much shorter that when they are picked up, they will found to be what is called "long teeth."

The Best Grinders.—The most popular way of grinding is with a wheel about five or six inches in diameter, having a five-inch face. This grinder, when in what is termed good running order, does capital work, but the time it takes to do it in, is somewhat to its disadvantage. For instance, in grinding a thirty-six inch cylinder

with this wheel, one-seventh of the surface is all that is touched at any time during the traverse. Hence, although the card is well ground, the time consumed by the work is something that carders fret over. Still, if it can be afforded at all, the superior sharpening accomplished by this make of emery grinders fully warrants, and in most cases repays, the loss of time.

The other kind of grinder most generally in use is what is designated the roller grinder. It is five inches in diameter and one inch and a-half longer than the width of the cylinder. This over-reach is allowed for the traverse. On account of the work done by this grinder being continuous, and therefore at least six times faster than the narrow wheel, it is often preferred. In competent hands, excellent sharpening can be executed with either sort; still the narrow wheel is the favorite where the ruling desire is not to save time.

Leather and wooden strickels, and other appliances of the kind, are often used in emergencies, but are never to be recommended, because they strain the wire and grind the card off the true, the result of which is nitty carding at certain points where otherwise the work is good.

Covering Grinders.—Our first duty is to make sure that the tools with which the grinding, setting, or clothing is done are in such order

as will insure "well set-up" teeth and true cylinders. The grinders should be properly covered, true-running and in good condition otherwise. A faithful index of the manner in which the cards are kept, is to be found in the thoroughness exhibited in caring for the tools. To cover or relay a grinder so as to insure first-class results, requires that careful attention should be given to the emery, the lapping of the wheel and the handling of the glue. The emery being mostly dusty, ought to be washed in clean hot water. In such case the old emery washed off the wheels previously may be added, as the boiling water will dissolve whatever glue or oily matter may be still in it. The water ought to be changed until it remains clear. Put the emery away to dry in a clean, warm place.

Wind spinner's banding tightly and evenly around the wheel. Be sure that both ends are well secured. Soak over night the glue in vinegar instead of water. Prepare it very warm, and with a good body put it on very evenly over the wheel with a brush. Keep the wheel turning all the time, and when all is ready hold the hot emery high over the wheel and drop it on so evenly and carefully that every part will be covered as it passes. Keep turning slowly until the glue sets. In order to keep out moisture, or oil, the grinders ought to be kept in a clean, warm,

covered in place. They should also be sponged every week with turpentine, so that the full cutting qualities of the emery may be secured.

Putting the Grinder on the Card.—There are a few points essential to safe and successful grinding, which it will be in order to call attention to here. It is well known that there are whole cylinders of clothing rendered worthless on account of accidents which happen when the cards are being ground. To prevent these, more than ordinary caution must be taken. In the first place, let the doffer be drawn back from the cylinder about one quarter of an inch. This is for the purpose of allowing space sufficient to set the doffer to the grinder and to be safe from rubbing the cylinder, a circumstance which must be prevented. That is to say, by drawing the doffer back, we afford room for the wheel to be set lower down, so that the peripheries of both cylinders will come in contact with it, and the cylinders will run clear of each other.

It is very important now to see to the "tightening-up" bolts and "adjusting screws" of the "doffer," for a good many accidents are the consequence of these being neglected. If the adjusting screws are forced to put the doffer back, without the tightening-up bolts being loosened, as they sometimes are, something is likely to be strained or broken, which takes such a long time

to repair that the operator will use his ingenuity to make it "go" until a more convenient opportunity. These screws and bolts being intended to hold the doffer in position, are needed most when the said doffer is revolving at 500 or 600 revolutions, and ought, therefore, to be carefully seen to, as should also be the bolts with which the "grinder stands" are bound to the card frame. If these do not fit exactly, the high speed at which the wheel is driven will surely shake them loose, and the result will be similar to that of a badly fastened "doffer."

The belts by which the grinder is driven must be very neatly lapped so that no tug or jerk may be felt while running. It is of great utility that these belts be of sufficient tension to maintain a regular speed, but not so tight as to shake the stands and cause the wheel to bump against the cylinder. Every card-grinder is well acquainted with the effects which follow the "grinder" getting out of place, and has spent many weary hours in the endeavor to "set back" the teeth so as to make decent work, but without avail. The result in every case is shovel-edged wire such as is seen in the cuts on the succeeding pages, of teeth spoiled by the grinder, and which invariably produces nitty carding.

Good Grinding.—The sharpening power of an emery grinder is its peripheric velocity added

to that of the cylinder with which it comes in contact. And the traverse is the difference between the revolutions of the shell and the screw. These data are taken from a full length grinder; but the power of a wheel, according to the same rule, would be as much less as its width would divide into the width of the cylinder. This theory is certaintly not correct; if so, a five-inch face emery wheel would take seven hours to grind a 36 inch card, which the roller grinder would do in one hour. Long experience has proved that a good wheel will do at least half as much work as a good roller grinder. It will make sharper and more perfect points on the wire, and save time, by making it necessary to brush less to get rid of the hook. (See cut on succeeding pages: well-ground teeth unbrushed).

But it matters not (as both patterns of grinders will do good work) which we are operating on. The science of the one is the science of the other. Let the wheel be level, brought to the distance of a thick gauge at both ends of the cylinder, and the set-screws on the back of the slides made pretty tight. Follow up with the doffer to the same gauge, run the wheel across a time or two, to make sure that all is clear. Put on the belts, and start the engine up slowly.

A small quantity of oil will be necessary, but not enough to spatter on the clothing. Set

lightly to the cylinder first, and bring the doffer to bear afterwards. After running a couple of hours, stop the card and ascertain how the grinder is acting on the parts which have been blunted through rubbing. If the glaze on the wire is not being sharpened, the wheel may be set a little closer. But it will not do to be setting up the wheel to the wire often, for the best carding edge, and the most free from hook, is that on which the grinder cuts itself almost clear.

There may be some parts of the blistered clothing recently drawn up which have been made hollow by rubbing against the feed-rolls, top-flats, and doffer; or, if we are operating on a roller card, against the licker-in, rollers, and clearers; but it is not necessary to keep the grinder running until these are ground out. This would incur too much wear of clothing for such small results, unless it should happen that the sheets are all redrawn. Then it is incumbent that they be as well ground as when the card is newly clothed.

The traverse or lateral movement of the wheel prevents a flat edge, so that when a cylinder is well sharpened it will feel perfectly smooth both ways.

A brush with good long bristles is a part of the card grinder's " kit," and, after the grinder is taken off, should be used lightly on the cylin-

ders for as much as ten minutes. This is very
effective in removing the hook from the wire,
and when the card is started the fibre will comb
much freer from the doffer.

The licker-in, generally clothed with hardened
steel wire, is a very particular cylinder to grind
in such a way that there will be no hooked or
ragged edge; for if there is, it will not remain in
good form for any length of time, but will get
choked up so as to be very damaging to the
carding. It should be allowed to remain grinding until it is perfectly smooth, both roundwise
and crosswise, after which it should be thoroughly
brushed, either by circular or hand brush, set
and tried, and if it will not clean it should be
brushed again until the cotton is delivered to the
cylinder free from sticking. (See cuts at
end of this chapter of well-ground and brushed
teeth).

The care of top-flats.—The teeth of the
top-flats ought to be "run" with the card-knife
tubed straight into line, and ground and brushed
to a perfect edge, by the time the cylinder and
doffer are ready. From the hard usage the top-
flats receive from the automatic strippers, the
teeth are often found to be laid in a very irregular manner. Being in this state interferes greatly
with their usefulness in straightening the passing
fibres, and shows the value of having them at-

tended to and put in position every time the card is ground. If a flat sheet be met with, the teeth of which are maintaining their regular form, and standing up well to the work for which they are designed, it is not absolutely necessary that the knife be run through them. The portions of the wire laid down and tangled are quite sufficient to be manipulated with the tool, because this continuous running is found in time so to loosen the teeth in the foundations, that when at work they do not stand against the "pull" in their orginal or best carding form, but give back so as to be almost straight. This, instead of drawing, the fibres parallel with each other as much as possible, allows them to pass on in a far from satisfactory state. A flat is sometimes discovered so hollow in the centre, that it cannot be ground true, except by reducing the teeth at the ends. The cause of this is generally the warping of the wood and the remedy is to take the sheet off and have it " trued up."

The top-flat clothing table.—The top-flat clothing table is of special service to the man who knows how, yet it is seldom kept in such a state that a flat can be put on and reclothed, or drawn up, without some trouble in putting it in serviceable order. This is, perhaps, the worst neglected piece of mechanism in the card-room. It consists of a strong frame set up in a conven-

ient place for light, with bar, ratchet and pliers attached. The flat-seat is made full length and nearly the depth of the flat, with the front or breast-piece well rounded off for the pliers, and with clasps to fit over the ends of the flat to hold it in position. This tool is generally home-made, and many original ideas are developed in the construction of it, which no doubt could be improved if builders of card-room machinery were to take hold of it. But the principle point is to keep it always ready, to save time ; and then small jobs will be done at once, which, on account of the condition in which it is kept, are often neglected until they become extremely hurtful to the work.

Card Setting.—The style of the engine determines the manner in which it is to be set. The eye, the ear and the guage are often all brought into requisition before the various carding points are properly adjusted. Correct setting becomes each year of more consequence, on account of the increasing demand for perfect yarn. Especially is this so when the carding is for fine numbers. There are so many machines in the market for carding cotton all of which have their good setting points, that it is no easy matter to determine which is the most proficient. The many antiquated ideas which are being burnished anew and put into more effective settings

by the aid of improved construction, make one conclude that the advancement in carding cotton is not due so much to recent scientific research as to the perfection of the mechanical means for making all appliances more effectual.

There are but few serviceable devices on the cotton card of to-day that were not in operation forty years ago. What is the railway-head but an extension of the old-fashioned "doubler," where from two to four slivers were condensed into one? A combination of rollers and top-flats has been in operation, and, for numbers up to 36s, has proved a more than ordinarily good card. Extractors of every conceivable shape have been applied to cylinders, and operated with more or less advantage for as great a length of time. Revolving flats, cards doffed with rollers instead of combs, cards feeding back and front at the same time, two slivers delivered from separate doffers, from the same cylinder, shell feeds, centre-pressed feeds, feed-rollers covered with card-clothing, self-strippers, brush-strippers, fancy rollers, draw-boxes, coilers, knife-edge plates set with screws, steel knives inserted between rollers underneath the cylinders of front feed cards, cylinder screens, solid, perforated and slatted in every possible form and width of space —all these for the purpose of preserving the staple, multiplying the setting points, and ren-

dering the card more effective as a single machine.

It will be seen from these numerous devices that the " setting " is one of the most particular operations belonging to the business of the card grinder. He must study what is of practical and positive efficiency in attachments, and the particular purposes for which they are intended, so as to produce the best effects in actual operation. The common top-flats, on account of the manner in which they are gradually widened from doffer to feed, set bevelling, so that the front of the flat be twice as far from the cylinder as the back, are all that is ever allowed to be measured by sight, and that only for the purpose of determining the bevel; for the back must be gauged in the same way as the feed-rolls, or doffer.

Where the space to be measured is from the ninetieth to one hundredth part of an inch, the unaided sight alone is not a sufficient guide. By the use of a steel gauge the utmost exactness can be attained, as well as the greatest possible safety to the clothing, and the certainty of regular and protracted production. The gauge then must be used everywhere in " setting " the parts together in working position, in bringing the different points to the closest possible clearance, and to ascertain definitely whether the cylinders and flats have been ground true or not. A well-made card, suit-

able for fine cottons, can be set to No. 33 gauge, and when so set will produce splendid work.

The card grinder must always bear in mind that the feed rolls, to make uniform work ought to be set so that the cylinder or licker-in will "nip the staple clean, without any lapping or appearance of fibres dragging, or turning over the rolls." In adjusting the "flats" he must understand that the fibre is, by the action of the cylinder teeth, made to slide from one to the other, and that the movement of the cotton is checked by the teeth of the flat, until it is laid, fibre by fibre, as it passes onward. Hence the necessity for having top-flats set bevelling, gradually widening in front towards the feed-rolls. This space well proportioned materially increases the efficiency of the card. Rollers and cleanersshould be set as close as possible without being allowed to rub. These doff and feed on to the cylinder alternately.

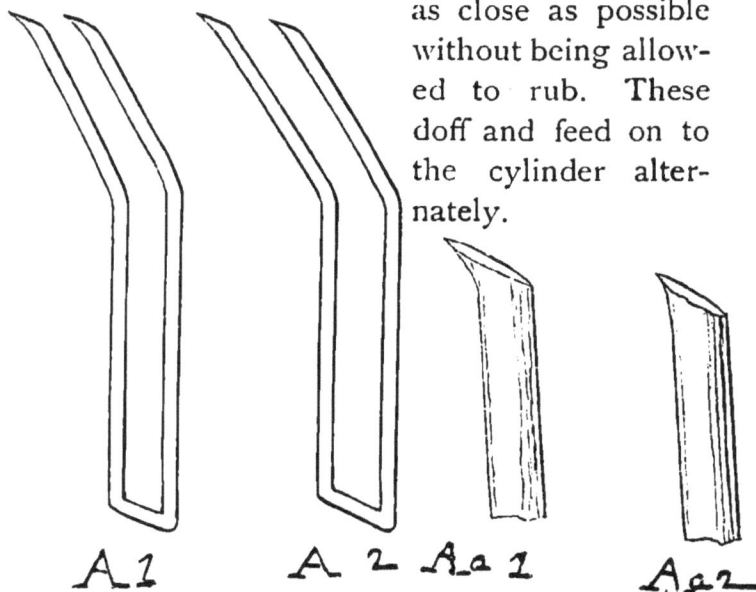

A 1 A 2 A a 1 A a 2

A 1 represents wire from the top-flat, well-ground and brushed ; and Aa 1 represents the same wire much more largely magnified.

A 2 represents the top-flat wire well-ground, but not brushed ; and Aa 2, shows the same wire more largely magnified.

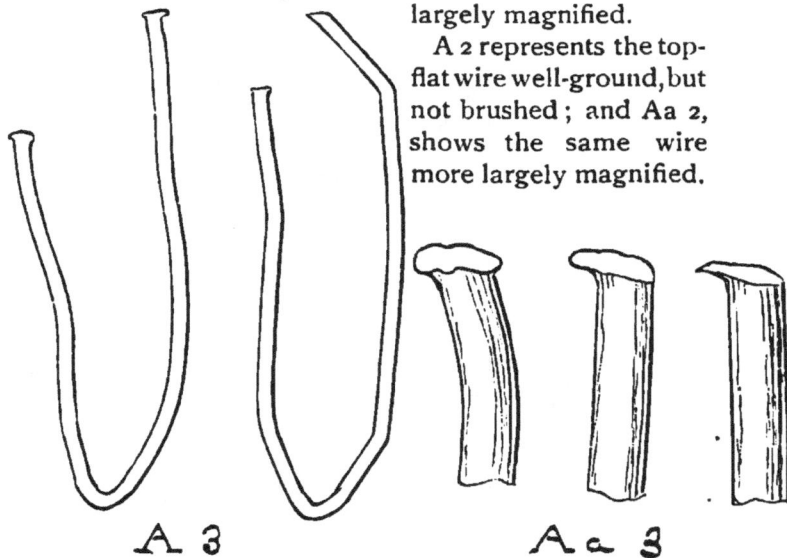

A 3

Aa 3

In A 3 we have top-flat wire so treated as to have been spoiled, and the particular effects of bad grinding are more distinctly shown in the enlargement of the same points in Aa 3.

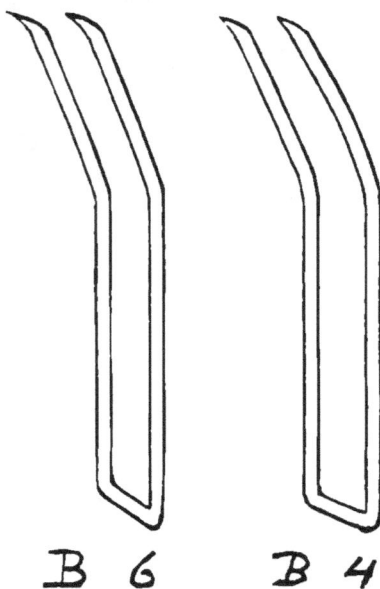

B6 6

B6 4

B 6

B 4

In B 4 we have cylinder wire ground and not brushed, while Bb 4 is an enlargement of the point of the same wire.

In B 6 we have cylinder wire well-ground and brushed, and in Bb 6 the enlarged point of the same wire.

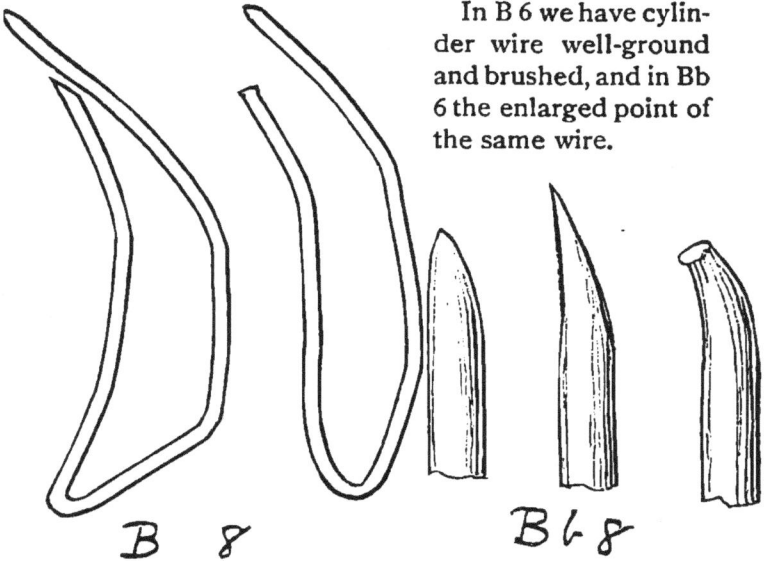

B 8

Bb 8

In B 8 we have cylinder wire badly spoiled in the grinding, and the effects of the maltreatment are more plainly shown in Bb 8 an enlargement of the points of the said wire.

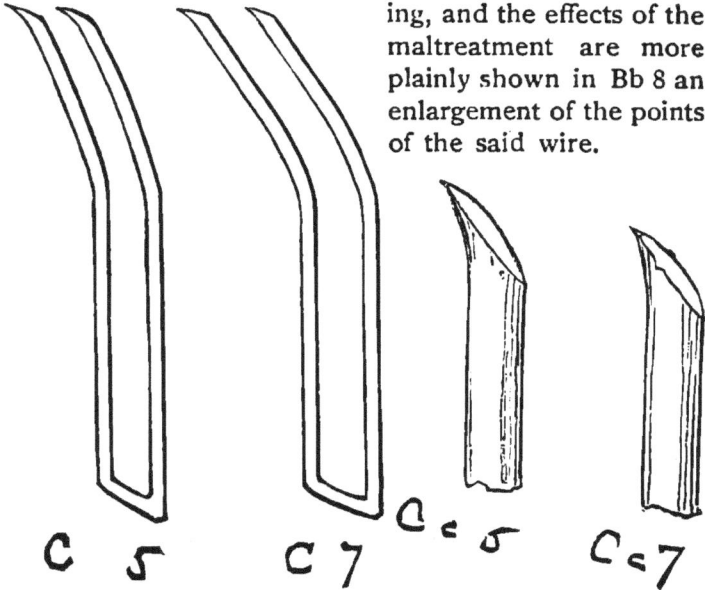

C 5

C 7

Cc 5

Cc 7

C 5 shows wire from the doffer well ground and brushed; while Cc 5 is the point of the doffer wire greatly magnified.

C 7 represents the doffer wire ground but not brushed, and Cc 7 is an enlargement of the point.

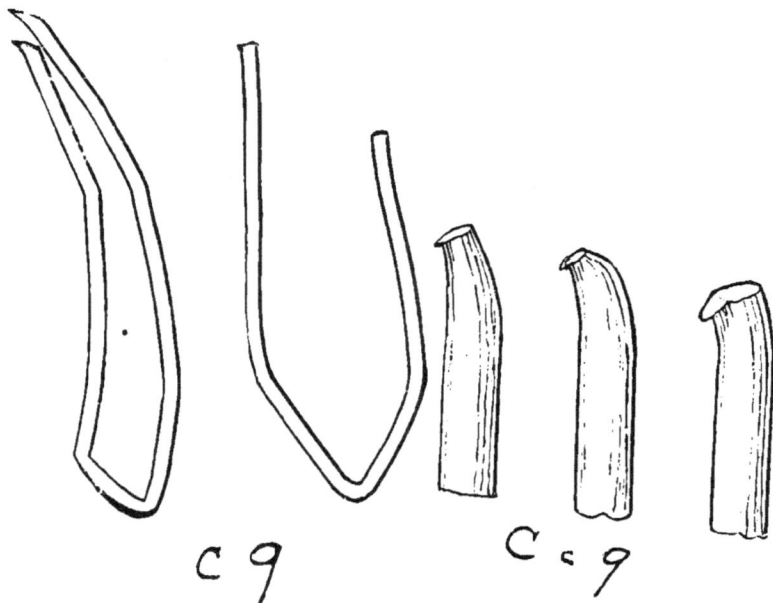

C 9   C c 9

C 9 is an illustration of the effects of bad grinding upon the wire from the doffer, and Cc 9 shows the results upon the points much more largely magnified.

CHAPTER IV.

THE SLIVER.

Importance of even delivery draw-boxes,

—Having considered the conditions of the card wire, the grinding and the setting, it will now be in order to trace the delivery of the sliver after being combed from the doffer and compressed through a trumpet. The question to consider is 1. Do the cards work singly or in sections? 2. If operated singly, are they using the draw-box with fluted under, and leather top rolls geared for a draft, of from one and a half to three? The en- gines fitted with draw-boxes are mostly of the roller and clearer type, and are chiefly operated on the coarser grades of product where large production only is profitable.

Although these draw-boxes are often neces- sary for the purpose of reducing the sliver before being doubled four into one at the drawing, yet

they cannot be trusted to make even work for any length of time. Placed in a position where the rollers must be driven at a great speed, the least bit of cotton getting under the saddle-bearings will cause them to cut the sliver, thus making many piecings and much waste at the drawing.

Of all the places in the card-room for drawing cotton, the draw-box attached to the front of the card is the worst, because it cannot get proper attendance, and the consequence always is a great amount of waste. What is wanted from a card that works single is a strong, even sliver that will pull out of the can from the bottom without either breaking or straining, so as to cause no piecings or fine places, which cannot be taken out after and must surely appear in the yarn. It has been found to be an advantage in the matter of getting better and cheaper work, to take these " draw-boxes " off, and alter the speed so as to run the sliver direct from the trumpet and condensing rolls into a revolving can.

The Necessity for Uniform Weight.— All the cards that work for one drawing frame ought to have a sliver of uniform weight. One yard of sliver from each card should be measured off and weighed, and the others should not vary from these more than two or three grains. This may be done at every change of laps, and if it is found that the same cards are heavy all the time

it may be concluded that the drafts are not all alike. This must be seen to at once, and all the draft-gears counted and made precisely of the same number. But the cards may not all be of the same make, and then may require different pinions to produce the same draft, owing to other parts not being similar. Still, to produce uniform weight the drafts must be made the same.

In weighing these slivers, if it should be found that they come sometimes heavy and sometimes light from the same card, then the fault lies in the laps, which are not as regular as they ought to be. A platform scale in the lapper room is the remedy for this. On it every lap as it comes from the machine ought to be weighed until it balances at the proper point, or at least does not vary over half a pound. By attending to this a few times a day the operator can prove whether the evener is running as it should or not, and if so, there will be no trouble in keeping the weight right. The carder may occasionally test the laps himself. If this matter be well attended to, there will be but little trouble in keeping the numbers even afterwards.

The Coiler.—The weight of the sliver, and the best method of condensing it for drawing, are next to be considered. In a carding room a sufficient number of engines should be allowed to keep up the supply of carding without being from

time to time compelled to meet the demand by adding weight. The weight of the yard of sliver, from the same cards and for similar counts, takes a wide range in the various mills. Some mills card 75 grains to the yard, while others run as low as 50 grains. Some use coilers and others railway heads. Now on a card, that is to say a common top-flat, which produces 75 grains of sliver per yard, and condenses it in a coiler, there must be but indifferent work. It is altogether too heavy and the coiler makes it still worse. Not only is the machine pressed too hard, but a twist is also put in the sliver, which makes it hard for the drawing rollers to draw, with the result that the drawing sliver will be hacked and the yarn will be very uneven.

These are the first and main points to look at for the making of smooth, even yarn. Coilers must necessarily have their condensing rollers so tightly sprung together that they will drive the sliver through the coiling gear. This, and the twist they give the strand, make a heavy bulk of cotton, too hard to draw. Still, coilers are extensively used on coarse numbers, where imperfections are not so visible. But for fine yarns, where the thread must be strong and level, considering that the fibre has to be drawn to its utmost, the coiler is a machine which ought not to be employed.

The coiler, however, has its good points. The can being the best-filled and containing the greatest quantity, is by far the most reliable and runs the longest, and, as a result there are less piecings and stoppages. Another point in favor of the coiler is that on coarse " counts " it generally receives but the production of one card, and, therefore, cannot contain singles or make large quantities of waste, like doubles or railway heads. There can be no doubt that if there were any device by which the twists could be taken out of the coiled ends before they enter the drawing, the effectiveness of the coiler would be increased, and as a means of filling cans it would be still more largely employed.

The Railway Head.—The railway head is another, and some think, a more efficient device for concentrating the carding at a given point. It is a most important machine, and on it depends greatly the quality of the goods produced, as well as the regularity of the spinning. It should therefore receive close attention. The weights should hang straight, the levers should stand parallel with the beam, and the conducting pins at the back should be as close as possible to the rollers. The slivers ought not to be contracted any more than just enough to prevent feather-edges on the front roller. The up-take must be computed to such a nicety as to prevent the slightest drag be-

tween the card front and the railway back. There should be no back-play in the shipper-screw to prevent the " evener " from acting quickly. The cone-belt ought to be level and of the best material. The rollers, on account of the heaviness of the weights, require strict attention, and want to be varnished often. If there should be the slightest curl-up of the sliver these rollers must be set a little wider. Should thick and thin places appear they must be moved a little closer. These and the driving-belt of the back portion of the head, the pitch of the gears, and the manner in which the slivers from the doffers enter on the belt, all have an important part in making the railway head keep up to the standard of. work. If we are sure these various things are in good order, and kept so, we may rest satisfied that the complaints regarding the running of the work in other departments will be few. These are the things which we can help, and if we are not watchful of them we are neglecting our duty.

But there are other things connected with the railway head which we cannot help, and which to some make it objectionable. In the first place, the evener is on the wrong side of the machine, so that a number of inches of sliver must pass before the evening is effected. This cannot be prevented any further than that the nearer we keep the machine and all its parts to perfection,

the shorter will be the length that passes. Again, if the piece upon which the evener is called to act be short, it will pass without regulation, while a certain length of that following, which is in all probability the right weight, will receive the action of the evener, and be, therefore, made heavier or lighter, as the case may be, thus doubling the evil, and causing twice the length of sliver to pass in irregular shape.

A bunch sometimes will pull the trumpet down and throw the belt an inch or so along the cones, which will be making light work until it returns to the proper place. A thin part will do the same in the opposite direction, so the " railway-head " is not quite as it should be yet. All this unevenness would be averted if some genius should place the " evener " behind the head ; and recent information says that this is being accomplished. Our railway arrangement is a good and cheap one for almost all numbers spun without combing, and barring these defects, is a perfect machine.

—

CHAPTER V.

THE DIFFERENT VARIETIES OF CARDING ENGINES—BACK-FEED AND FRONT FEED—THE WELLMAN STRIPPER CARD—THE REVOLVING FLAT—THE ROLLER CARD.

Back-feed Cards.—It is not the purpose of the writer to express a preference for cards of any particular model or to claim that his experience in carding is worth more than that of others. He merely wishes to indicate his own practice during a series of years in this especial field of cotton manufacture. Having had charge of, and operated, cards with back-feed and cards with front-feed, cards which were hand-stripped and cards which were self-stripped, cards with rollers and clearers and cards with revolving flats, he thinks he is qualified to form a just opinion and to offer substantial reasons why certain kinds of engines are best adapted to, and more profitable to operate upon, certain grades of stock. Twenty-five years ago he was carding all kinds of cotton, and for all counts up to 200s. and even higher, on cards the cylinders of which were thirty inches in diameter and the doffers thirteen

inches. These were back-feed cards and they made a good record for quality, but were deficient in quantity of product. Numbers of these machines are still running, however, on combed yarns and giving good satisfaction.

Front-feed Cards.—Then were introduced the front-feed cards, which at first and until, comparatively speaking, a recent period, were a decided failure, especially on the finer grades. This no doubt was mainly attributable to the manner in which the cylinders were inclosed beneath, as no knife plate, or contrivance of any kind, could be brought with like effect so near the periphery as the flats. Besides this the elevation of the doffer excluded all chance of having more carding area, or introducing more flats. Hence, while the cotton passed from the feed-rolls to the first top-flat, the centrifugal force loosened the cotton on the cylinder to such an extent that there was always more than the short and seed thrown on the flats. This, together with the production of an extra quantity of flies, of a very superior kind, which necessarily must fall from a card of this description, was a great hindrance at first to the popularity of the front-feed engines. But this difficulty has been removed in such a thorough manner that on the modern front-feed card the flats are brought near to the rolls, with the effect to obviate those

faults entirely. This improvement has made cards which feed at the front, or under the doffer, very acceptable for all kinds of numbers, and the mechanical intricacies, at one time thought so inconvenient, have been simplified to such an extent as to make the machines very close competitors with the revolving flat cards, even for carding select combed yarns.

Licker-in and Carrier.—By the introduction of the "licker-in" and "carrier" to the modern front-feed card, there are brought together other good points for separating and ejecting the foreign matter. In these cards the licker-in is made to strike downwards, and the feed rollers are pitched so that the under is the setting roller and affords a marked advantage to exude the seeds and sand at this point, while another appliance, called an "extractor" increases the effectiveness under the centre line.

The "carrier" revolves in an opposite direction with as much more superficial velocity as is requisite to strip the fleece from the licker-in, while the cylinder, at a still higher speed, strips the carrier in the same manner. By this system of feeding we secure a downward blow for the cylinder, as well as the licker-in, thus offering additional facilities to clear the fibre by the force of gravity.

If we examine the direction given to the cotton, by this method of feeding, and the recent

improvements introduced, to assist in the extraction of the motes at this most accessible place, we can discover how well adapted this style of card is to the lower and softer grades of cotton and the reason why it is so much preferred by spinners for coarse counts. The pernicious system of overloading has become so prevalent with spinners of these counts, that the good points on the cards are seldom secured. Large production and reduced attention are the conditions upon which these engines are run at the present time, so that the advantages of construction have little to do with the quality of the work.

The Wellman Stripper Card.—There are really but two principles involved in the construction of cotton cards, which may be simply designated the flat and the roller. The principle of the flat is a succession of narrow carding surfaces retained in close proximity to the cylinder, through the wire of which the cotton is teased along and straightened out by the action of the cylinder, while in the wire of said flats various impurities and foreign matter lodge until removed by the stripper. On this principle we have the top-flat, the under-flat, and the revolving-flat. The American manufacturer long ago adopted the top-flat as the best for carding cotton. When Mr. Leigh, who spent many years trying to in-

vent a top-stripper, saw and studied the principle of the Wellman attachment, he unhesitatingly admitted it to be the carding-engine of the future. And we think were it now put on the market for the first time it would be a very desirable and acceptable machine for all purposes, as indeed from the range of work it is doing it has proved to be. All admit that the cards which take out the most matter foreign to the yarn with the least loss of prime fibre are those upon which we accomplish the best results. When we lift the flats off the Wellman engine we cannot fail to observe the large amount of blighted seeds and short staple those next the feed-rolls contain, and how these impurities, though less in bulk, but still numerous, lodge in the last, or flats behind the doffer. This is a feature, and a very commendable one, which no other cards but those of this type possess.

The common and under-flat cards are shown to advantage when the strips are compared with even those of the revolving-flat. It is found, especially where the quick automatic is used, that they take out more dirt, seed, and short dead fibre, and prove that there are cleaning points in this card which have not yet been beaten. The essential difference, then, between the steady, and the revolving-flat is that the one is dragged over the cylinder, while the other is lifted from its

position to be stripped. There is no other improvement on the one which cannot be equally well applied to the other. If a cylinder 50 inches by 40 inches, with other parts to correspond, is of any advantage, it is equally so in both. If shell feed and metallic lickers-in are desirable in the one, there is no reason why they should not be so in the other. In fact, every improved feature of the revolving-flat card can be utilized with equal advantage in the construction of the Wellman card. And so far as the flies, or drops, are concerned, there cannot be any great difference, because screens or grate bars can be equally well applied to both.

Of course under this head the Foss and Pevey card is considered, and we have not yet seen or operated a carding-engine which gives so much area for cleaning and produces better work with less waste. Besides, any one capable of forming an unbiassed opinion' knows from practical experience, that this purely American machine can produce 80 lbs. of carding per day of ten hours, with less power and expense than any other on the market, and this carding is superior and takes a wider range than almost any other.

The Revolving Flat Card.—It is not necessary for the writer to seek information regarding the revolving flat, or as it is now designated, the traveling flat card, because it was the machine at

which, from boy to manhood, he worked. Thirty-five years ago in one of the largest mills at that time in the world, it was carding cotton for 40s water twist, and 60s filling. While attempting to describe the points which characterize this carding engine, no injustice shall be done to the other side ; but we shall endeavor to clear away some of the rubbish and sentiment that interfere with the merits or demerits of an old machine.

It is said that in those days the construction of machinery for cotton-mills had not reached that point of development necessary to build such a complicated machine. Accuracy of workmanship and nicety of construction are absolutely requisite to the success of any machine in the factory as well as to that of the revolving flat card.

The cylinders of the card under consideration were of cast-iron, turned up, pierced for plugs, and they ran as perfectly true as any we have ever seen and at as high a velocity as those of the new models. These cylinders were clothed with Horsfall's patent clothing, which has a name second to none at the present day. The flats traversed a circuit concentric with the cylinder, and each one had screws by which to adjust it. The lickers-in were clothed with diamond-pointed wire, and each machine carded in ten hours 1 30 lbs. of cotton for the above mentioned counts. The flats were ground with

full length grinders and were brushed with circular brushes while working, so that no time was lost in stoppages. A man and a boy ground sixteen of those card cylinders and strickled and brushed the doffers in ten hours.

The cotton which these cards carded for 40s twists and 60s wefts would make one of our modern carders stare with wonder. The cylinders we see were ground just as much as they were in need of, once a day, and stripped after running five hours with a rapidly revolving circular brush, which was driven from a groove in the flange of the loose pulley, and held up in the same stands as the grinder.

Now how much does the modern traveling flat card exceed this of thirty-seven years ago? What recent improvements, or special mechanism, has been added to it that has brought it prominently before our manufacturers of late? If improvements have advanced in this machine, as it is asserted they have in others, the revolving flat engine of the present, must be a different card from the one at which we worked in 1854. There were difficulties encountered in building the old card which were hard to overcome, but which improved methods and tools, longer experience and greater resources, have been able to surmount, and for this reason the traveling flat card of to-day is a comparatively new machine. The chief

difficulty experienced at the time mentioned was in maintaining the circuit traveled by the flats concentric with the cylinder, and in the forming and fitting of the parts necessary to secure this result.

Formerly it was found very hard to get accurate mechanical construction in the upper surfaces of the bends. That the wire of the flats resting on the bends should be in even and very close proximity to the wire of the cylinder, and run true in this manner all the way round, was absolutely essential. Not only so, but there must be provision made by which this could be continually maintained to accomodate the wear of the wire. This was the principal difficulty presented in the construction of this card, and with this overcome, there is nothing about it that offers any obstacle in handling and caring for more than a common Wellman stripper engine.

The Roller Card.—In spite of the improvements so extensively advanced as having been added to the preparation departments, and especially to the cotton card, both at home and abroad during the last decade, what has been long known as the roller card has continued to fill an important place, and indeed hold its own, if not more, in numbers up to the medium. The principle of this card is essentially different from the common or traveling flat. It is built on the teasing and separating plan, and aspires to nothing it cannot

do, while it is operated on the very cheapest scale.

The cotton is fed to this card with the improved shell-feed. Then by a small cylinder it is lifted from the main cylinder, doffed by another still smaller cylinder, by which it is fed back into the main cylinder again, and this is repeated sixteen or more times before it reaches the doffer.

The roller card is not adapted to very fine work, but it is a popular machine in England on medium and coarse counts, because very little waste is made, there being no strippings taken out. On the best authority this card is stated to be doing 175 lbs. in ten hours, on 36s yarn, and making first-class work.

•   •

CHAPTER VI.

CARDING BLEACHED AND COLORED COTTON.

Troubles with Such Cotton.—In carding bleached and colored cotton, difficulties crop up now and again which are never so annoying when the material is worked in the natural state. Trouble may always be expected when the temperature is low, with a dry crisp air, and cold north winds are prevailing. Manufacturers have been known during periods of this kind to be compelled to stop operations until the return of more favorable temperature. Others under such circumstance were able to go right along, without suffering any more than the ordinary inconveniences of such weather, and without having occasion to use extraordinary means for keeping matters right. Now why should such differences exist? Why is it that one manufactory should go along so easily without trouble, and without having appliances

of any kind to overcome difficulties, while others with all kinds of attachments for averting the evils have the greatest trouble to get through the work ? This is the secret which we desire to unravel, and if we discover the causes which produce the effect, we may suggest how to counteract them, partially at least, and to a great extent remove the annoyance.

Different causes of Difficulties.—For many of the evils which are likely to arise in the carding of bleached or colored cottons, it is, we fear, impossible to point out a remedy. The many changes in the temperature that occur during the year ; the time that elapses after drying until the cotton is brought to the cards; and the manner in which it is handled previously, all combine to supply causes for annoyance at this particular place.

It is well understood that bleached and colored cottons absorb a deal more moisture than the ordinary fibres, and a continuous moderate temperature is the most favorable for carding them. It is, therefore, necessary that the factory should be on low ground, with a stream close by, and sheltered by hills on the north and east. The basement or cardroom should be as low as possible, and no air openings should be under the floor whereby cold currents may ascend. It is a very troublesome business to card cotton out of which the natural oil has been extracted by bleaching or otherwise.

Especially is this the case in a factory exposed to the full force of the northern winds, with the card-room above a sub-cellar, or with floors through which air-currents have free passage.

The character of the building and machinery are also powerful factors in making this kind of cotton. In the location described, the cold air often rushes with force through the crevices and openings, creating a strong upward current. It draws the fibre, when in a fleecy state, in all directions, divides the slivers on the railway and drawing heads, causing them to spread out and separate. Because these air-currents inflate the bleached and dyed fibres, the cotton will cling to the conductors and condensing roll. It no longer remains compact. It loses its affinity. It sticks to the edges and sides of the cans. It will not fall into the cans. In fact it cannot be pushed down in any good shape into them with the hand. The currents of cold air rushing upwards to displace the lighter and warmer air above, give the fleeces an upward tendency, which causes the fibres to spread and cling to everything around them. In carding the bleached and dyed fibres the air must be well impregnated with moisture.

Temperature and Moisture.—The dry-air from steam pipe heating lacks the moisture necessary to prevent this confusion, except at a temperature considerably lower than it is usually kept at

while the fibre in the natural state is being carded. Still in no case can it be dispensed with, in this climate at least. But it is often forced so high as to be unbearable to the operatives. When the weather outside is cold, as a remedy for sticky work the heat in the room is often raised to 90 degrees and more, while it is well known that common cotton cards and works best at between 70 and 75 degrees. In this case of colored and bleached fibre extreme heat will not help; it only aggravates the evils, and is therefore just the reverse of what is required, for the greater the heat in the room, the stronger will be the upward current of air. The proper way is to maintain the temperature at a minimum. Both night and day let the thermometer stand at about 65 degrees. The moisture will then average 60. Have three thermometers to try with, one near the floor, one near the ceiling, and one in the middle for the working test. The difference between the upper and lower will be the force of the upward current. If the difference is kept between one and two degrees, the working or middle thermometer may be as high as 68°. But there will be trouble if the upper and lower show a variation of from 6° to 8°.

Some carders have, with good results, had recourse to a system of heating the cans by steam pipes or other appliances, for the purpose of cre-

ating a downward draught. The object is to make the lower part of the can warm, and to cause the air at the upper part to fall with force, creating a downward current which will take the cotton with it. This method is considerably better than the system of blowing steam around the rollers, which causes everything to rust and does no good at all to the cardings. If the air is found to be too dry, very fine jets of steam might be allowed to issue on the north side of the building, as near the ceiling as possible, and perhaps ten feet apart, because to create a downward current the moistened air is valuable ; at least it is useful in checking or retarding the upward current and materially counteracts the cause of bad work.

In connection with this matter there are other things to be considered, such as the dyeing, the drying and the storing before the stock is presented to the card, as well as the mixing and the best method of obtaining bright colors.

The Effects of Light.—Though good light is essential for all kinds of carding, yet intense light is very injurious to colored work. Solid colors withstand the light better and fly apart less. With mixtures, or when white is used with a heavy color, it is very troublesome, because they have no affinity. The lighter color has a tendency to fly from the heavy, and intense rays

of light, as well as intense heat, increase the attractive power which draws the colors apart. When light penetrates with force, it may be subdued considerably by colored window curtains, or frosted glass. This will also contribute materially to preserving the color of the cotton, giving it a brighter tint and a better gloss, qualities very desirable to preserve, but on which the light has a bad effect. If these were all the advantages procured by having the light mellowed, they would be sufficient to recommend it, but there are others. There will be less waste made, less piecings of ends, less labor and more perfect work.

Artificial Light.—All the influences which make the work go badly in a mill with white cotton have doubled force in the mill running on colored work. Especially is there a harassing time when the machinery has been standing idle for a day or two. In such a case, good results may be obtained from lighting the gas for a couple of hours. The heat thus diffused has a softening influence on the atmosphere, and permits a certain amount of moisture, which steam heat does not give.

The effect of gas-light on the drawing of the cotton is very marked and favorable, especially when a wind storm springs up and scatters the fibres in all directions. By the aid of gas-light the effects may often be controlled, and the work

kept going right along. In exposed locations when sudden changes oftenest occur, use of gas-light is one of the best temporary expedients practiced. It gives heat and moisture combined, radiating from below, as well as from above, and giving no perceptible upward current.

Preserving the Color.—The saving effected in the working of cotton after coloring makes the practice desirable, but it is very difficult to obtain and preserve colors that will compare with those to be found in the dyed yarn. In many cases this kind of manufacture is carried on without the necessary amount of skill and knowledge, so that the endeavor to approximate to the nice shades and colors of the material that has been dyed in the yarn is not satisfactorily accomplished. The desire to have a good color is, of course, strong, and yet in many instances the extraordinary efforts to get it tend only to destroy the effect and to injure the work. During the carding, much of the coloring matter falls out, and the same thing occurs in the process of drawing and twisting, all of which hurts the color and ought to be avoided by proper methods in dyeing. It is absolute waste to load the material with unneeded quantities of dye. The fine fibres will only absorb a certain quantity of dye and any additional amount put on them is sure to go to waste. Carelessness in preparing the cotton for

the cards, and in loading it with more matter than is necessary, has a very injurious effect on the preservation of the colors.

Making dyed cotton ready for the cards. —The desideratum in preparing fibres of dyed cotton for the card is to have them free, and devoid of stickiness, so that they will not be badly torn, and the liability of the color to come out be increased. If the processes before reaching the cards are intelligently performed, that machine will be relieved of duties which do not properly belong to it. Bleached or dyed cotton should be stored away for a week or ten days, at the least, before carding. In this delay lies the cure for almost every evil incidental to the manufacture of this class of goods, as compared with the ordinary white goods. After the cotton is brought from the drier, it should not be packed tight; especially if only the stated number of days are to intervene before using. It should be laid on a floor where the air can circulate above, below, and around it, and the temperature should be kept steadily, night and day, at as near 65 degrees as possible, for the reason that if it is too dry it will absorb the proper quantity of moisture, and if too wet, it will part with the moisture with which it is overcharged. By having this rule closely observed the cotton will be brought as near as can be to its natural state.

If brought to the carding engine too dry, much of the color will be thrown off in combing the fibres, and it will appear dull and faded, and besides, dry, warm stock is always more likely to generate electricity. On the other hand, if the cotton be brought forward in its too wet condition it will not only lose color in the carding and drawing, but it will also destroy the card wire and produce a poor quality of work. So the very simple rules which indicate how to preserve the color in the best possible manner, also help to preserve the card clothing and to make the best work all round.

Faulty Dyeing.—There are no manufacturers of dyed yarns who do not desire to get at least moderately fast colors. There is great dissimilarity in the cotton manipulated by different dyers. Much depends on the facilities at their command, and a great deal upon the methods adopted in the work. A most important thing is the cleaning out of the vat, which should be done regularly and often. A desire to save may move the dyer to keep the old sediment for a large number of dyes. This may be properly called wasting, because in cotton there is a small percentage of natural oil which operates against the action of the dye and remains in the liquor, which, when used often, becomes overcharged and causes the material to feel greasy. When in this state,

the dye easily rubs off. The pressure of the rollers of the various machines will obliterate every vestige of the brightness, and by the time the cotton gets into the cloth it will look dingy, dull, and faded.

The way to get the best possible color with the least amount of dye, and to have at least moderately fast colors is the most economical. To make this sure, the vat ought to be cleaned out every time, and the liquor used as a mordant on the next vat following. Then use only once, after which let it pass away. By this method it takes rather less dye to set the vat, the colors are always regular and the cotton pleasant to the touch. This may be called the economy of dyeing fugitive colors, although in this system there is extra cost for the plant, for it requires two vats instead of one, to do it effectively. But it produces good results in the work afterwards, and gives a good appearance to the cloth.

We do not pretend to be competent to give instrutions in dyeing, but we do know when the work is badly done and that bad dyeing interferes greatly with good carding. Cotton having a greasy, "soggy" feel in handling, will not card well. It will not separate at the feed-rolls. It clogs on the wire ; the short fibres roll into minute balls, and make what is called a "nitty" sliver. A fleece of this carding, if held up to the light,

would seem to be full of small "nits," and in such a state it can never make good work.

Squeezing and Extracting.—Cotton that is wet lies inert; it has no spring or elasticity like wool, but without resistance remains just as it has been pressed. It is very desirable that the cotton should be kept as open as possible during the extracting, so that the process of drying may be forwarded with such uniformity as will insure good carding. Cotton squeezed through rolls under a heavy pressure is never in good condition for carding, because it is in slabby, hard-compressed pieces. The dryer will not open these to any appreciable extent, nor will the beater in the lapper entirely do so, and when presented to the card in this irregular state, the wire although of the best tempered steel, sharpened and set in the most approved fashion, will not produce good even work. From poor carding, all the other evils follow, such as uneven yarn, bad spinning, and large quantities of waste at each operation. The flies and strips from the cards, when on stock of this description, are double what they ought to be. It is nonsense to try to make work out of lumpy material, and when the water is pressed out with rollers cotton is always lumpy after being dried. Some portions, which receive more pressure than the rest, come through in shining cakes, glistening like

silver. These spots are not taken out by all the machines combined, and they often appear in the cloth in such numbers that they cannot be "burled" out. Rollers also press out the coloring and produce a variety of shades to the same lot of material, which when worked up on the picker and card give anything but a true color.

It will be observed from these remarks that good hydro-extracting is, for this kind of material, the only sure way in which to keep it spongy, so that the air will circulate, and be distributed all through the mass drying it with uniformity and in a condition to preserve the brilliancy of the colors.

The Importance of Proper Drying.—We have referred to this already, but it is of such importance that it ought to have a paragraph to itself. The cold-air method is the safest for this kind of material.

One of the most notable difficulties produced by over-drying is the development of electricity in the carding. It is generated, no doubt, to some extent by the heat with which the fibre is impregnated, and this is so tormenting and so certain to produce bad work that the cotton would be more profitable in the bale. These conditions can be obviated if the material is extracted without lumpiness and dried in the right

manner. If over-dried, the life and strength of the fibre are destroyed; for, although of great tenacity, it can be singed and have its vitality completely burned out. When hot-air drying is used, there should be an experienced hand to attend to it, for there may be some portions over-done and some under-done, the results of which will be as before-mentioned. With hot air much experience is required to tell when the cotton is dry enough; but when properly dried, and with reasonable facilities for storage, to give it a chance to "age" and return to the natural state, it will be found when wanted to be in as good a condition to work well, and with little more trouble than the common white stock.

The Use of Seed Extractors on the Cards. —In carding colored stock, every appliance known to have been used with success, in removing the specks and nits, should be adopted. The Keene extractor, the shell flat and the adjustable knife have their proper places here, and will be found to more than repay their use in a short time. In mixtures with black and white, or black and yellow, the smallest speck, or "nit," is plainly seen, and whether done in the vat or by the squeezing process, stands out very prominently. By the use of these appliances on the cards, the yarn and cloth of very opposite

colors are made clean in appearance and soft to the feel. The great point, therefore, in carding and spinning this kind of stock, is to let it "age," and so naturally return to its original state, without which it is not possible to get good carding and fast colors.

CHAPTER VII.

CARDING FOR COMBED YARNS.

SKILL REQUIRED FOR THIS PROCESS—GOOD MACHINERY NEEDED—POINTS THAT MUST BE LOOKED AFTER—THOROUGH CARDING CALLED FOR—USE OF THE DRAWING-HEAD COILERS.

Skill Required.—There is no process in cotton spinning less frequently discussed than that of making combed yarns, nor is there one in which so much skill is required to make the operation successful. Very few not directly engaged in it realize the amount of extra labor, caution and cleanliness necessary to keep the yarn up to the standard. One thing is in favor of the carder for these counts : He does not have to contend with the unknown constituents of a lower grade, but has always honest and well-selected material to handle.

Good Machinery Needed.—As there is but the single process allowed in all concerns when combed yarns are made it is very essential that the cards shall be first-rate in every respect. The clothing of the cylinders and flats must be composed of the best material. The wire must

be of hardened and tempered steel, so as to insure the desired elasticity and a better and more
lasting point, thus permitting harder usage and
withstanding the excess of stress necessitated by
the carding of the longer staple. Hardened and
tempered steel wire has now greatest popularity,
and is almost universally used for fine carding.
The flat card system has been accepted everywhere as the best for carding Egyptian, Sea Isl-
and or Peeler cottons. The material demanded
for the class of yarn under consideration will not
admit of being teased and disunited in a rough
way. It must be combed over the ends and
drawn into parallel fibres by the means best
known to the carder. By feeding slowly to the
periphery of a well-clothed cylinder, running at
a moderate velocity, and by using the feed with
the most tenacious grip, we have the kind of
machine most desirable for this work. We also
want the flat which will take out the most dirt,
and at the same time draw the fibre best into
line. Hence it is the flats, and the methods by
which they are actuated, which secure preference
for the principles involved in the flat carding
system.

The arrangements for setting the flats at a perfectly graduated slant from one end of the circuit to the other, and the positive manner in
which they are held to their duty, are wonder-

fully free from defect. Each flat, with certain motion, travels over in closest proximity to the cylinder, wire to wire, without touching; the whole space occupied by the full set. The clean flat enters upon its work behind the doffer, and finishes it at the feed-rolls. This continual motion tends greatly to draw the staple into line, and to straighten it, thus giving a degree of excellence to the carding that few other machines can impart to long-stapled stock. The feed is set a little under, in order to allow the periphery of the cylinder to come nearer to the nip of the fibre. This is where the draft of the card is, and here the straightening process takes place. By the set of the feed, and the quality and sharpness of the wire, the crossed fibres are the better reduced.

At this place the extractor is now in operation with the best results. It sets very nicely to the cylinder, and its sensitiveness recommends it. It is a mote-catcher that once seen will be summoned to the aid of the card working for combed yarns.

Stationary flats do their duty well. They, too, are extractors, holding to the periphery of the cylinder, a one-and-a-half inch face, slightly raised at the edge next the impact, for the purpose of catching the short and foreign matter which the centrifugal force throws off. These

faced flats are therefore very little, if any, inferior to the most improved traveling flats for the purpose of producing well-carded and well-straightened cotton, for combed yarns, except it be in the quantity carded.

This is the kind of card and the sort of carding which is most desirable for the best yarns, and in order to give the machines the greatest chance to produce such work, we dispense with the licker-in. Here an almost indispensable adjunct on the coarse grades is not allowed. A great egester of seeds and motes, a great opener of stock, and a saver of clothing is not considered profitable for Sea Island cotton, or other long-stapled material, because it prevents the cylinder to a large extent from straightening and laying the fibres.

That the wire on the cylinder does straighten the fibres better when brought into immediate contact with the feed, is a fact which all who have attempted an analysis of the science of carding will admit. Wide set feed-rolls cause the cotton to lap around the one from which the cylinder bites, and instead of the fibres being properly laid on, they trail, as it were, and get into small bunches, thus missing the efficiency of the process partly, if not altogether. The laps on these rolls often become so hard, when carding long stock, that the teeth of the clothing

will get set back with serious injury to the wire.

The doffer is, scientifically speaking, for the purpose of collecting the fibres from the cylinder and delivering them at a specified weight. But in order that the doffer may perform this function in a satisfactory manner, it must be set in such close proximity to the cylinder as to be just clear. Now, if a blister, or some other imperfection, makes necessary the withdrawal of that doffer from its most effective seat, what will the consequences be? In the first place, the doffer will begin to deliver a lighter quantity, and in the next place, the cylinder will retain, for some time at least, the fibre which the doffer ought to be delivering. But in a short time the cylinder will have more than it can carry, when the cotton will begin to nit by rolling and the centrifugal force will throw it in every possible direction. These are extreme cases, to be sure, and easily attended to. But there lie between the perfect working card and these extremes, certain particulars incidental to minute degrees of setting, which are not so readily watched and guarded against, and the attending to which marks the successful carder of fine stock.

Points to be looked after.—Clothing should be drawn and nailed on by a thoroughly practical man, who understands just what is wanted,

because regularity of stretch prevents blisters. Still it is possible to run cards so close that the best stretched clothing will spring and blister. An ill-set jam may have the same effect, and cause the same trouble. A bungled jam may be even worse than a blister, for the teeth may be so loosened in the bottom as to lose their elasticity. It may set them to leaning both ways, according to the pressure, standing neither against the cotton nor the grinder, but straightening out with the centrifugal force and making bad and nitty carding.

The nit in coarse numbers does not show so prominently as when the thread is drawn out to a very fine count. Here it stands out in bold relief and carries its evils with it, all of which are attributed to inefficiency in the carding.

These nits are not found uniformly distributed through the whole of the carding, but are most numerous in cards of the above description, or before stripping or sharpening time. The cause of this is the fact, that the longer the card is allowed to run, the heavier will be the accumulation of strip, and the more likelihood there is for the cotton to roll between the points of the teeth.

Of course the better the condition the card is in, the more surely the nits will be reduced both in size and number. Still, in carding stock suitable for fine yarns, it is a very difficult matter to

keep the work clear of nits. In fact it is not effected at all without the aid of the combing machine.

Thorough Carding Necessary.—It has been said that the passing of the cotton once through the cards is sufficient, when combing machines are used, because these will deal with the shorts and motes while the combs will take out all the rest required. Still, an object to be aimed at is to have the material in proper condition, before presenting it to the combs; and the method of doing this in the most practical as well as the most economical form. Before the advent of combs we were compelled to continue carding the staple until it was free from every speck that would in anyway be detrimental to the yarn. This was very weakening to the fibre and caused great trouble in the after process, and was the source from which came the large quantities of waste that went back to the pickers. The combs have obviated all this and they do the cleaning much better than any cards possibly could.

Use of the Drawing-head.—But there is still another condition of efficiency to be noted here which tends to the progressive evening of the fibres lengthways, and diminishes to some extent the weakening effects resulting from carding doubles. It has always been found in practice to be expedient to run the cotton once and sometimes

twice through the drawing-head, as a very useful help in doing what the cards leave undone in the way of evening and laying the staple in the same direction. When it is understood that the combing machine requires the cotton to be laid lengthways as much as possible, in order that the nippers may catch it in the most advantageous position, it will be seen that the idea of elongating by drawing was a very natural one.

Coilers.—Coilers are not so numerous in fine mills now as they were ten years ago. They were extensively used at first, but small defects were found which were hard to remedy. These decreased the desire to have them, and in spite of the beauty of their workmanship and excellence in can-filling, they are not gaining ground.

Beater-Speeds.—In mills where fine yarns are a specialty a very perceptible difference in the beater-speeds will be found in the picker-rooms. The velocity must be proportioned to the length of the staple. Long-stapled cottons have an economical point of beater-speed somewhere, which, like the twist of roving, is learned only by experience. It has been demonstrated by a series of experiments, carried on under very favorable circumstances, that the correct limit of beater-speed for long-stapled stock is between seventeen and eighteen hundred revolutions of the ordinary double bladed perforated beater.

The Sectional Evener possesses very superior gripping power, and is therefore well adapted for fine cottons, because long stock is more subject to be pulled in bunches. This is prevented to a great extent by the manner in which the rollers of the evener are constructed, so as to hold the cotton with double power.

CHAPTER VIII.

COMBING THE COTTON FIBRE.

THE COMBING MACHINE—FINE YARNS MUST BE COMBED—
THE NIPPER AND COMB SYSTEM—CAPACITY OF THE COMB
—COMBER-WASTE—WEAR AND REPAIR—THE NUMBER OF
THE NEEDLES—THE SLIVER—CAM MOTIONS—DRAFT AND
WEIGHT OF LAPS—RULES FOR SETTING THE COMBS.

The Combing Machines.—The changes effected in the preparation of fine counts by the introduction of the combing machine are surprising. That machine embodies ideas of distinct originality, in the development of which several mechanical difficulties are made to harmonize. Here the cam-motions are made exclusively practical, and show with what concise regularity they may be made to bring fibre to fibre. The finest needle-pointed tempered steel wire is required for these combs. This preparatory process is of a delicate and complicated character, and on every detail of it much depends. It has been reserved for this age to complete and introduce an invention which takes hold of the cotton fibre in a natural way and sends it to the spinner in a state which far surpasses anything of the kind previously known.

It is a complex contrivance, to be sure, and has been a long time making its way to favor among manufacturers, but those who spin fine numbers now realize that they cannot get along without it.

Fine Yarns must be Combed.—The combing machines have now been in operation long enough to have stood the test of experiment, to which inventions brought for the first time into practical use are necessarily subjected. There can be no question, in spite of some differences of opinion, that fine spinners have reached the conclusion that they cannot succeed without them. The preparing of the cotton for the spinner is a perplexing problem, which often confounds the wisest man. The more we are pressed for quantity, the heavier the carding must be made, and the more deterioration of the quality is aggravated. But the machine under consideration is so sensitive in every particular that to push it hard will deprive it of efficiency with fine numbers Its capacity for separating the short fibre from the long, and for evening and straightening it at the same time, is a sufficient warrant of its real practical utility.

The Nipper and Comb System.—The features of this machine are the nipper and comb method, by which the nits and broken seeds, with the fine hairy feelers or prongs that reach out in all

directions and intertwine with such persistency, are effectually dissevered and removed, and the healthy fibre sent forward in a perfectly clean and purified condition. It is then ready to be drawn out to any degree of fineness, for the purpose of making thread, or to be woven into cambric without spot or blemish. The picker and the card, and we might safely include the gin also, have a tendency to split and deteriorate the fibre, and to reduce its strength considerably. By the way which they are constructed they cannot but cross and tangle the fibres; but in the combing machine the impurities are carried over the ends by the needles, in a manner which is perfectly natural, and better calculated to even and lay the staple in a parallel state than to injure it. In fact, from the way in which it is drawn by the combs, it cannot be otherwise than inclined in the same direction.

The capacity of the Comb.—A machine that can be adjusted to take out from five to forty per cent. of the fibre, according to the length desired for the numbers, must be applicable to a wide range of work. This scope is not half developed yet, but in time it will be fully employed in kinds of manufacture which requires just a certain length of staple and which no other machine can supply with nearly the same exactitude. Besides, there are classes of goods which cannot be made soft

or silky to the feel with the present preparation, but when combed, fibres are found to spin with less twist and to make a much softer cloth with a gloss and beauty after calendering and finishing which are far ahead of anything the cards can do in this line. The manner in which cotton cloth that requires brilliancy of color and soft, fleecy facing is now made must be departed from, and the combs brought into action to prepare the stock, because superior work and clean soft cloth are always secured from combed yarns. A manufacturer also knows just what he is going to get from the combs and can depend upon receiving it in the shape required.

Comber Waste.—It must not be forgotten that the short or noils thrown off by the doffers from the combs are from what is considered an extremely good class of cotton and are therefore much sought after to manufacture into coarse yarns. These shorts command a fair price and make the strongest quality of a coarse grade of goods. Buyers know that this cotton is carded before it is brought to the comber and cannot on this account be foul. This, together with the fact of its coming from a superior class of stock, makes it sought for, and it always commands a ready sale. An industry like this is very profitable, and is sure to be established in any locality where there are sufficient combs to make it an object.

Wear and Repair.—There is one more point which it may be proper to consider in connection with the combing machine and its properties for work, and that is the wear and tear. Some machinery is very costly to keep in such order as will ensure the desired results; especially is this so with regard to the carding engine. No machine requires more care or more outlay to keep it in perfect order than the one first mentioned. The comb, however, does not require any great outlay on furnishings. To be sure it wants to be set regularly, and the comb teeth now and again must be renewed. This is cheaply and easily done, often, when there are not a large number of machines, by the carder himself. A place is appointed for the repairing of the combs where the special tools required for the purpose are kept. After the broken needle-points are taken out, and the place in which they were is cleared of the old solder and cleaned of every speck of oily matter, it is thorougly tinned over, and the steel points, according to the number, lifted with a magnet and placed the proper distance apart. After this a little acid is applied and then a hot soldering-iron with a very little solder is run across lightly. This closes up the interstices between the needles and sets them firmly in place. Great care must be taken to clean and brush the combs after this, because the acid will

rust them and make trouble afterwards about the work.   .

The Number of the Needles.—The needles of the combs are made of tempered steel wire and of the following numbers.   .

From one to six comb.	22 wire.
" seven " nine	24 "
" ten " eleven	26 "
" twelve " thirteen	28 "
" fourteen to fifteen	30 "
" sixteen " seventeen	33 "
and top " comb	28 "

The top comb rests in front of the cushion-plate, and is the last set of needles through which the cotton passes.   Here, then, are seventeen rows of combs, composed of different sizes of wire, all of which are drawn through every fibre, on the same principle as with the familiar process of combing the hair.   Indeed it is said, and we doubt not with considerable truthfulness, that the idea originated from this.   But, be this as it may, the idea is the only natural one we have ever seen put in practice to take the impurities out of cotton.

Improved Machines.—The nipper holds the one end of the fibre against the cushion, and the rolls the other, until alternately the combs pass through both ways.   The improved machines are adapted to comb both ends of the

staple with the cylinder, while the older ones dress but one end with the cylinder, and the other with one, or sometimes two, top combs. These latter machines seem to make a considerable advance in the proper direction, and will tend to make the comb more popular on this account. These machines have longer cylinders with two comb sections, and two fluted sections, and a double grooved cam to correspond.

Disjointed and Pieced-up Slivers.—A disjointing of the sliver is the result of each turn of the cylinder, a circumstance which cannot as yet be avoided on account of the combs being constructed to carry the motes, nits, and short over the ends of the sound staple when held between nipper and cushion. The rolls therefore have to return part-way back, at each revolution of the cylinder, in order to piece up and deliver a connected sliver. The distance the rolls have to return must be nicely adjusted, or else irregular and hacked slivers will be delivered and the work will prove uneven and break so that large quanities of waste will have to be made. It is part of the business of a carder who runs combs to see that the motion of the rolls backwards is so geared that the inaccuracies resulting from this continuous break and splice of the sliver are scarcely noticable. These continual piecings are a serious drawback, and no doubt any

remedy looking to an uninterrupted delivery of a combed sliver would be an escape from needless work.

Cam-Motions. — A very peculiar action in the mechanism of the comb takes place in the back-turn of the rolls for the purpose of re-uniting the sliver. The seventeen rows of combs, when set in the cylinder, occupy somewhat less than one-half of the circumference, and the remaining part is intentionally left vacant. When the needles pass through the fibres of the sliver held out to them, the cushion and nipper fall into this vacancy and permit the rolls without rubbing to return and piece up.

The cam and ball which operate this movement must be watched and kept without play, because the slightest digression from the positive direction is the source of great trouble and long stoppages. In fact, anywhere on this machine where two distinct motions are made to take up the same space alternately, particular care must be taken with the cams and balls. The latter must be tempered hard, and made a good, easy fit all round the cam. There being no other machine in the carding-room where the cam and ball are brought into action so much as in the one referred to, it is therefore necessary that the operator shall get thoroughly acquainted with this part of the work and never forget, when putting

in a new ball, to feel it with the fingers all round the groove. This is important in practice, as cams are often burst because these small things are not being looked to in time. On a combing machine head there is complicated work, some of which is pretty hard to get at, so that when an accident occurs from some small neglect there is often a large amount of work to be done for the necessary repairs.

The Prevention of Weak Work.—To make the weak parts disappear from the combed sliver, a much greater number of doublings is necessary than is really good for the work. Still, these must be resorted to for the purpose of reducing the cloudiness. This is a delicate operation to do well, to avoid waste, and not to stretch the sliver so as to make it uneven. The feebleness of the sliver delivered from the combs necessitates such a loose release from the rolls that there is always a danger of lumping or bunching under the condensing rolls. The operator, therefore, has to be continually on the alert for this, and at the same time to make sure that the polished table on which the ends double and pass along to the can-head or coiler, as the case may be, is always free from any damp or sticky substance which would cause them to adhere and make a break in the doubling. A considerable amount of valuable waste is often made at this place, and

nothing must be neglected, even to the slightest detail, to keep it down.

The Draft and Weight of Laps.—The total draft of a combing machine with the draw-box is about 16; that is to say, one inch going in at the back or feed rolls comes out at the coiler 16 inches. The laps are generally six in number to a machine. Some have only four. Others again have eight; but six is the average and the lap generally weighs from 160 to 200 grains per yard. We have had combs running with a lap 194 grains per yard, six laps to a machine; that is 1164 grains per yard feeding at the back or feed-rolls and when it entered the coiler it weighed but 65 grains to the yard, with a loss by combing in waste and noils of 17 per cent.

Essentials to be Remembered when Drafting.—In drafting a combing machine it is essential to bear in mind that the index-gear and the cam-shaft both run at the same velocity. The index-gear is on the cylinder shaft, and with a pin attached to it drives the feeding rolls, and the gear on the end of the cam-shaft the delivering rolls. The ratchet-gear, which drives the detaching shaft and front rolls, is also driven by the cam-shaft, one turn of which makes one tooth of the ratchet. In working out the rule for drafting, which will be given in another chapter, it will be necessary to remember that the

notched gear makes four turns for one of the ratchet.

Rules for Setting the Comb.—The following rules are generally used for setting a Hetherington comb for long Sea-island cotton; but these may be slightly modified to advantage on other grades : Lever or catch to fall in at $1\frac{3}{8}$; lever or catch to fall out at $10\frac{3}{8}$. Commence to feed in at $4\frac{7}{8}$. Detaching roll to touch circle plate, or the fluted part of comb cylinder at $6\frac{3}{8}$. Nipper to touch cushion plate at $8\frac{5}{8}$. Leave off drawing at $9\frac{1}{2}$. Drop top comb at $6\frac{1}{4}$.

Another Rule used on Egyptian Stock.—Cylinder to gauge at 5.25. Catch to fall in at fully 1.3. Catch to fall out at 13.25. Top comb down at 7.1 ; Cushion plate up at 5.1. Nippers meet at 9.75. Detaching roller down at 7.1. Detaching roller up at 10. Feed to begin at 10.56. Top comb to set as close as possible. These points are all shown on the index-gear, and can be understood after considerable practice.

CHAPTER IX.

DOUBLING AND DRAWING THE SLIVER.

Few or Many Doublings.—There are carders who recommend few doublings for the purpose of producing an even sliver; but they by no means make it clear why it is they would discard an old and tried system. Few practical men would advocate an innovation of this kind without having special reasons therefor. "In nine cases out of ten," says one of these overseers," uneven-ness is produced in the drawing." Wherein, then, is the use of all the exactness resorted to in the carding, in order to make the work straight and clean, if it is made uneven the moment it enters the drawing rolls? And why is it that, as a remedy, we should be advised to take out a doubling? The answer to these questions is to be found in our improved quantity-producing

cards, or, to be more exact, in the manner in which they are operated, as will be seen.

A Case in Point.—A room with 60 cards of the old pattern, and 5 railway heads, 12 cards to the section, is calculated to card sufficient to run the spindles. These cards are thrown out, and 24 of the large-producing kind put in. Now, the first-named machines kept two grinders busily engaged to maintain them in good working trim. But when the new style machines were set to work, one grinder was dismissed on account of the small number of cards to care for and the other one was intrusted with the charge of grinding and setting the whole. These 24 cards were driven so that they actually produced more work than the 60 old ones did; and all this weight of sliver was forced through three railway heads. The weight necessary to hang on the rolls, to draw in any kind of fair shape the concentrated slivers of eight of these cards, is sufficient to keep the top rolls almost the whole time in poor condition. Indeed, the best covered rolls are seldom able to withstand the compression required to sustain the weight of slivers to be drawn on these railway heads. This is seen to the best advantage when we clean and set the head in order and put in a complete set of new rollers. It at once becomes apparent that the machine is working smoother, for the

irregularities which were caused by the bad rolls, and which kept the trumpet bobbing and restless all the time, are not there.

This illustration shows without doubt that the leather rolls are the source from which the uneven work springs. At the time the railway head was introduced, double carding with light sliver was the accepted method, which afforded and does still afford, where this system has not been thrown out, a much better chance for the head to draw well and the "evener" to correct with more regularity. We cannot conceive of anything more out of line with the progress of cotton preparing than to set down a railway-head and evener to draw and correct the size of eight or even more cards of the improved and prolific class designed for single carding, especially for the coarser counts.

It must not be understood, however, that we find fault with the new cards, for when compared with the old they are in many respects superior, if the grinding and setting are attended to with intelligence. And here we desire again to say that the heavy amount of carding these new machines are designed to do, and the high speed at which they are driven, make extraordinary care and frequent adjusting essential to maintain their proficiency. But this is what is wrong with the railway-heads. This is the cause of the uneven-

ness which our carders are complaining about, and it is likely to remain until common sense again assumes control and the English system of carding for coarse numbers is adopted. Let every card fill its own can, and make up the doublings by running the sliver lightly the necessary number of times through the drawing frame. In this plan there are no heavy ends to draw, and therefore no uneven work.

Imperfections in Drawing. — Imperfections in drawing may be somewhat modified by soft condensing and spreading the slivers well on the rollers. The card slivers should be equally distributed on the belt in the railway-box, so that they pass through the rolls in a thin and even sheet. Thick ridges caused by the ends entering the rolls, one upon another, raise the rolls unequally and cause cloudy drawing. Defects such as these, which make the work slightly hacked and lumpy, some imagine are of little account and will afterwards be leveled up by the doublings. This theory will not stand the test of experience, for no amount of doublings will amend the weak parts. They are only lengthened by the drafts to which they are subjected. Besides, it is the worst kind of workmanship to allow inaccuracies of any description that can be prevented to be passed from one process to another. Inequalities caused by the

evener, or rollers of the railway head, or in fact by any other rollers from whatever agency, will undoubtedly appear in the yarn. In doubling, weak places cannot be prevented from coming together, and when it is considered to what length a half inch at the first drawing process will be stretched when it reaches the last twist, we can form some idea as to the causes of uneven yarn.

Setting Rollers.—On a fair grade of cotton from ¼ to ⅜ of an inch is a good testing distance to set the drawing rollers apart, because there is no rule by which to govern this but by the rule of experience. Let it be understood that the closer we get the front and the next roll to it (for in every machine these two rolls do all the drafting), the better and more uniform will be the work. Still, this may be overdone, and the resistance may become so great as to cause the top rollers to slip and to be the source of considerable mischief. It is the slight slips that give the most trouble, because they escape observation, and we may be led to believe that the rollers are seated at the best distance while another sixteenth of an inch would remedy everything. This can only be found out by trial and experiment. The rollers will turn with more certainty, because the pull is easier, when set farther off; yet if they are set farther

apart than the length of the fibre they will pull fine places in the sliver which will be very detrimental to the yarn. The correct principle,therefore, is to keep the front and middle rolls as close as possible without crimping, and good spinning will always be the result.

Perfect Drawing.—The system of drawing by degrees on the same machine produces cloudy work, and there are reasons for this of a very cogent nature. If the volume of cotton is not properly contracted, condensed and adjusted while it is undergoing a series of drawings on the same head, the more it is drawn the more uneven it becomes. The custom is to keep the front leather rolls in good condition, while those at the back are old and often fluted. Between these the less is drawn the better for the yarn. Practical experience has demonstrated that on any machine operated for the purpose of evening and reducing the sliver, there is no place where good drawing can be accomplished but between the front and middle rolls. A light draft on the first head with few doublings is preferable to a more numerous quantity which would necessitate a heavy draft to keep down the weight. When we ascertain the manner by which these fine filaments are made parallel by drawing, we cannot fail to see that the method of connected drawing by degrees on the same head, misses the

object for which the drawing frame is intended. Contracting so as to prevent the edges of the slivers from spreading or "feathering" is the true principle of preparing cotton on the drawing frame. Perfect drawing is a cloudless and straightened sliver having a glossy luster, which if we do not secure on the finishing head, we have not attained the perfection which the machine is capable of.

Extra Doublings not always best.—It is understood when additional doublings are put in that an extension of the drafts is also made in order to counteract the extra weight. The object of these doublings is to mix and even the stock better while the drawing renders the fibres more parallel, and both of these operations are utilized to reduce the sliver to a proper condition and size for the spinner. This is the theory, but it is often modified to meet circumstances. Although the draft is not computed by the number of doublings, but from the weight of cotton passing through the rollers, yet it must always be in proportion to the hank sliver being made. Therefore, when we add doublings we must regulate the drafts accordingly. It is not to be inferred from what has been advanced, that all we have to do is to compute the doublings and drafts, and set the machine to work without considering how it is otherwise adapted to the class of stock we are

called to manipulate. It is at times like these, when changes are being made, that the wisdom of the carder is exhibited. A class of cotton with unequal fibres will not, under the same treatment, bring out the same quantity from the same weight, as would stock with a uniform staple. The carder must also remember that it is an untwisted sliver with which he is contending, and that equal doublings, on account of this inequality, will not stand equal drafts. As the fibres become more parallel the short releases itself and by repeated drawing, in this case, makes a lumpy sliver. So it would be better, before going too far, to turn it over to the " slubber," where a closer bite can be given it, and a little twist put in, which has been proved to be the best and most judicious way of operating on this description of stock.

A Drawing-Frame with the Most Advantages.—Cotton spinners have for many years been working towards the use of drawing-frames with a somewhat longer boss on the rollers, and the practice of using several bosses, separating the slivers at the back and concentrating them immediately in front of the trumpet inside the condensing rolls, has been dying out. This is desirable on many accounts. With long-stapled cotton a roller of larger diameter can be used; but with certain mixtures we find a neces-

sity for more latitude in the adjustment of the rollers, which with a smaller diameter and adjustable stands can be readily obtained. This cannot be overestimated, and it is a good sign of progress to see that some builders are adopting to a certain extent this line of practice.

This make of frame has every facility for accurate work so arranged that there is no collision or multiplicity of parts. It is built so as to be run three, four, five or six into one, according to the ideas of the spinner. Each one of the rollers is independently weighted on either end of the roll, doing away with the saddle-stirrup and the rocking motion of the roll being made greater upon one end and less upon the other end of the double boss. Back and front stop-motions are arranged so that it is impossible for laps or break-backs to occur to any extent. The calender rolls may be plain or grooved. The can tables are driven by an upright shaft from the bottom of the calender roll, and the same shaft also by means of the worm and gear system drives a transverse motion at the back. The system of weighting adopted is that known as the direct.

The gearing has been arranged so as to give the best possible results, as well as the greatest facility in changing. The difference between doubling at the back, where it should be done, and doubling with the old system of two bosses

in front, is simply that fewer edges are put together. The draft is upon a single sliver, rather than upon two, while the fleece of cotton passing and receiving draft between the rolls, is not liable to be affected by any deficiencies that may exist by means of different diameters in the bosses. Some of these little things are worth studying, for they make a great deal of difference in a machine for drawing cotton.

The Importance of Can-filling. — The filling of the cans is another of those processes demanding dexterity. No hand should be allowed to press down the drawing except one that has been trained to it, because the least catch or tangle will cause breakages and stoppages, numerous piecings, poor work and small production. The several devices at work for the purpose of filling the can show how essential it is that the sliver be pressed down in such a way that it will not break in the pulling out. It must not even be racked or strained in the cans. There never were better-filled cans than when they were gently pressed down by a slow-working plunger. There was no strain then in draw-it out. The can revolved very slowly, not more than six times a minute, though it is still better to have the can go only half-way around and back again. Coilers may be run to advantage where coarse yarn is made.

CHAPTER X.

DRAWING AND TWISTING.

THE SLUBBER—WEAK POINTS IN THE SLIVER—REMEDIES FOR
THEM—SLUBBER DRAFT REGULATION AND ROLLER SET-
TING—THE TENSION OF THE ENDS—TAMPERING WITH
THE LET-OFF—THE USE AND ABUSE OF DOUBLINGS—TRUE
· ROLLERS TO SPEEDERS—THE COMPOUND MOTION EXPLAINED
—IMPORTANT CONSIDERATIONS REGARDING IT—DUTY PER-
FORMED BY THE CONES.

The Slubber.—The slubbing is the next
process of interest that engages the attention of
the carder. Here he is compelled to enter upon
a new experience. With continued extension of
the fibre, the strength of the sliver is giving out;
so a machine is brought into operation which
will reduce it still more and preserve its uniformity. Hitherto no twist has been necessary, but
the reducing and equalizing on the drawing
make it indispensable . that a little shall be put in
to insure cohesion. In operating a slubber the
first thing to do (and it requires skill) is to get
the slivers up out of the drawing-cans without
racking or attenuating them. This may be accomplished best by setting the cans well in under

the lifting roller. By so doing we avoid the friction incidental to the slanting and rubbing against the edges. When we see the slivers back of the slubber falling back into the cans, and refusing on account of weakness or some other cause to continue the process, we may be sure there is something the matter that will require careful investigation.

There are a number of things that may be the cause of this. The drawing rolls may not be properly adjusted. If this is so in the last process, the weak parts will be separated but a short distance; but if they occur further back they will be much further apart. This is a practical way of locating faults. All the overseer has got to do is to give his attention to the distance these tender parts are separated, and by looking to the drafts to which they have been subjected, he may determine where the trouble is.

Other Reasons for Breaking Down.— Still, there are other reasons for this breaking down behind the slubber. It frequently happens that the drawing is running with an allowance of draft between the front and condensing rolls for the purpose of keeping the sliver taut. When running on heavy work, although some inquiry is done, yet through the strength imparted by the extra weight the damage may be imperceptible. But let us change to a lighter class of work, and

the slivers probably will not bear to be pulled up out of the cans. Let us get one tooth (often two will be required) more for the condensing roll and note what a difference is made. If the sliver is strengthened by the change we may congratulate ourselves upon having practically straightened out a part of the process, which was not as it should be. The surfaces of the front and condensing rolls should run exactly at the same speed. Be it remembered that the stock is made as nearly parallel by drawing on the pre-ceeding machinery as is prudent, for the sliver must have consistency sufficient to sustain its own weight. Still, before twist is given, there is another draft to be added. Thus it will be seen, that care and skill must be used at this extreme stage to prevent over-drawing.

We have been persistent in this chapter in directing attention to this point, knowing how important it is, and how easily too much draft may be given to the slubber.

Slubber Draft Regulation and Roller Setting.—Experience has demonstrated that the most economical machinery on which to draw cotton should have but three rollers with just sufficient draft between the back and middle to prevent the sliver from bagging. The reason for this is that the slower the roller which grasps the fibre moves the greater the chance the drawing or re-

volving roller has to make the work uniform. If we divide the draft between the front and middle and back and middle equally, we must of course speed up the middle rolls and these would naturally lose their retaining tendency and allow the cotton to give out in flakes, thus causing uneven and consequently weak yarn. The more we speed up the centre roller the more certain it is to yield the fibre to the pull of the next roll, the periphery of which is traveling at a velocity of three, four, and often on speeders as high as seven to one. Now this slower motion is just as capable of receiving the inaccuracies coming to it, as would be the velocity coming to it where the whole draft is given between the front and middle rolls, but let it be understood that the light drafts must receive faster and thus produce inferior work.

It must also be remembered that no yarn of good quality can be produced if we slub with wide rolls ; and this is a part of the business of carders and spinners that is to our knowledge greatly neglected. What is the use of all the trouble consequent on the shifting of the rolls for one sixteenth of an inch ? says a carder. But we know the closing or opening of the rolls that distance has often done wonders in making the yarn both to spin better and to break stronger.

The Tension of the Ends.—The tension of the ends on the speeders should be very light, so that the least possible strain can be felt when touching them with the finger underneath. There should be just sufficient tension to reach the flyers without too much hanging. If there should be any drag, it will surely twist at the rollers. It is common to see the speeder-ends, especially those of the slubber, so tight that they pull with the strain and make tender places in the roving. Have the twist light and the tension easy to produce good drawing on the next machine, is good advice. Hard twist may keep the ends from breaking, but it draws badly on the following frame, and cuts and hollows the leather rolls. If there are any tender places arising from poor drawing, wide rolls, or uneven feeding in of waste on the pickers, the twist running up into the bite of the rollers will pinch these most. Some of these places occur at irregular intervals according to how the doublings acted on them in the previous processes.

Tampering with the Let-off.—The remarks regarding tension stand good for all kinds of speeders, whether on coarse or fine hank. The retarding or tightening of the let-off is another of those small affairs which are productive of consequences of which the operator may not be aware, but which often take consid-

erable ingenuity to trace out. The system of "thumbing" the roll is bad enough, but not nearly so injurious as that of tightening. Let us take a frame on which we find a number of slack ends and set the rack to suit them; what effect has this operation on the other and much larger number of ends which were running at the proper tension? Will these break down? No; but they will pull and tug until they equalize the diameters of the bobbins by tighter winding. The loose ends to which we refer have been made so by neglecting to piece up in time, so that the bobbins are somewhat less in diameter. Now, the wind-on, having but the same length of delivery, must of course strain and tug at the roving to accommodate the greater circumference upon which it has to be wound, and this tension affects the weaker parts; for it is well understood that if we pull a piece of roving, the tenderest portion will stretch. Therefore attenuations formed by pulling down or tightening the ends are very slender and feeble, but not so much so that they will break down(except in extreme cases) either on the frame or in the creels, because they, so to speak, swallow up the twist which strengthens them sufficiently for future mischief.

We are referring to one only of the many things in the building of a set of roving which will cause weak parts, such as neglected rollers,

unequal pressures, or a poor cone-belt. But this tightening circumstance may and does frequently happen after the overseer has spent hours of his time tempering the machine and putting it in shape for first class-work. He is therefore off his guard, and in passing, if he finds the machine running, he takes no further notice of it.

An Illustration.—In order to illustrate our position regarding weak parts on the slub (and they are most frequently made here), we will assume the draft on the intermediate to be 4.5, that of the finishing speeder 7.5, and the draft of spinning-frame 8.5, which is a fair ratio of drafts to give these machines in ordinary practice. Now, by multiplying these drafts together, we obtain a product of 267.75, or if we allow for contraction by twist, we have 266. A single half-inch of a weak piece of roving made on the slubber will, therefore, be lengthened on the yarn to 266 half-inches. So we see by actual demonstration that the tender parts made on the roving by tightening, or from any other cause, however short these may appear at the machine upon which they are made, will under ordinary circumstances be an aggravating length when they come to be woven, and whether they appear in the warps or filling must give poor results.

Doublings, of which there are generally two, one on the intermediate and another on the fine speeder, help to lessen this degree of weakness somewhat, but there are chances remaining that two of these slender pieces may come together in the process of doubling, a circumstance that aggravates the evil. Besides, these same machines are subject to the same abuse. The frames upon which the remedy is being applied are liable to be tightened, too, and the consequences are of the same nature, although not so far drawn out. On account of their closeness to the spinning, the weaknesses will be the shorter, but none the less hurtful.

The Use and Abuse of Doublings.—From what has been observed in describing the failings of speeders and those attending them, it is not to be inferred that doublings are of no value in the preparation of roving. The writer has invariably maintained, in the face of opposition from practical men, that the factory which runs the most doublings produces the best work, provided the stock and machinery are equal. But doublings are like drafts: they must, to be effective, be judiciously applied, and not be the cause of weighty drawing on any of the machines to which they are put in process. Our idea has always been, and no reason has yet appeared sufficient to alter it, that if heavy, and therefore

cloudy and bunchy, drawing is the outcome of stuffing in doublings for the purpose of having as large a number as possible, a considerable reduction of these would be productive of better work and stronger yarn.

The Importance of True Rolls on Speeders.—Seeing that we are at present dealing with the speeder, our object will be to offer such suggestions as will not be disappointing to any who will take the trouble of putting them to the test. One of the first things to do is to look closely into the condition of the steel rolls, on which we are going to make roving. Put a straight edge along the bearings, and prove to your own satisfaction that these are perfectly level and that the journals will bear equally the whole length of the machine. Calliper the rolls in several places and satisfy yourself that they are sufficiently near, so that there will be no possibility of one of those troubles after starting which no person can account for. If the machine is old, see that the joints do not make a quarter turn, and that the flutings are not gone or hollowed down where they are in constant contact with the cotton. The rolls must be sharpened so that the edges of the flutes will offer equal resistance to the drag, and that there will be no uncertainty about the slip or escape of the fibre when brought under for the purpose of reducing.

Observe that there is no wabble to the rolls, caused from springing or misplaced joints, because that means uneven roving and lots of it. If the top rolls are solid be very particular that they are of the same diameter. This is often the source of much annoyance and irregular work. If the front rolls are shells, the diameters will not make so much difference, and in this respect they are preferable; but particular care must be taken of the spindle as regards cleaning and oiling.

The next and one of the principal things to look after is the weighting, and to this in a great measure is due the quality of the production. The saddles ought to be of a good pattern, and the friction reduced to a minimum by keeping the dents on them no larger than is serviceable. The stirrups must hang in such a way as not to rub the steel rolls, for rubbing not only wears the stirrup but causes misplacement of gravity; so will also a crooked stirrup, especially those kinds which pass through the weight.

The Compound Motion Explained.—In order that the compound motion on the speeder, and the methods of calculating it, may be explained and its significance as a movement understood and appreciated, let us offer here a few remarks concerning it. The first driver is a bevel, keyed or set-screwed on the main or twist shaft and

drives a pair of bevels in the interior of and carried round by the center-gear. Now, by the centre-gear carrying these double intermediates in the direction of the driver or fast bevel and in the contrary direction of the driven or loose bevel, it is evident that double the revolutions are taken from the last-mentioned bevel that the centre-gear makes. This compounding of fast and loose gears is for the purpose of regulating the wind-on of the roving in proportion to the increasing diameter of the bobbin. In the more recent arrangement of this motion, the centre-gear revolves in the same direction as the twist-shaft. The variation imparted to the bobbin side, is, therefore, two revolutions less than the centre-gear. But if the said gear revolves in the opposite direction it will gain in the same proportion. Hence the take-up is regulated by the centre-gear, and it in turn is regulated by the cones.

As the spindle and the bobbin revolve in the same direction, it is evident if both travel at the same speed no wind-on can take place, and it is also evident that if the bobbin remain stationary the wind-on will be equal to the length traversed by the flyer. As the twist is given to the roving by the spindle gaining a certain number of turns on the length delivered, so it is, by the spindle or the bobbin gaining on the length traversed by the other, that the roving is wound or lapped on,

hence the difference between the velocity of the spindle and that of the bobbin in either the new or old arrangement, is the wind-on, and must, at every stage, from the empty to the full bobbin, be equal to the length delivered from the front roller. But as each layer of roving enlarges the diameter of the bobbin, a little consideration will make it apparent that if the spindle and bobbin were to continue at the same velocity at each turn of the rail, more length would be required, or in other words, the wind-on would soon out-wind the length delivered. The effect of this continual increase is counteracted by the agency of the compound motion set to run in such a way as to cause the velocity of the bobbin to approach that of the spindle in exact proportion to the increasing thickness of the bobbin.

Important Considerations Regarding the Compound Motion.—When studying this motion at work, or computing problems relative thereto, it is necessary to bear in mind that the number of revolutions which the loose bevel is augmented or retarded is equal to twice the revolutions of the centre gear. And it is also very essential to know, when called upon to change any gears which will vary the speed of the centre-gear, that the slower said gear revolves the faster will the loose bevel revolve, and *vice versa.* Therefore, to give sufficient action to the compound

motion, the differential gradient which occurs at each turn of the rail must be so tempered by the let-off movement, that the bobbin will revolve exactly so as to wind on the length delivered from the front roll without drag. Of course the length delivered from the front roll is somewhat modified by the amount roving contracts in the twisting, and when exact calculations are requisite must be considered. And when two motions driven from independent sources, so to speak, are worked together for such a delicate operation as to wind on without drag or hurtful tension, exact computations are indispensable.

Another Duty Performed by the Cones.— Another use of the cones is for reducing the speed of the builder and equalizing the coils as the bobbin increases in diameter. As the bobbin enlarges, the rail must travel proportionately slow, and if the proper gears are supplied, this duty is performed with great accuracy by the cones. The gear that will start the ends loose enough on the first row, must be ascertained by computations. This is very important, for very often there is considerable drag, and consequently poor work is found here. The rail should at no time travel faster than just enough to allow the rovings to wind-on close enough to touch each other, because a wide coil-on allows the next row to get down into the space between the coils

and makes the machine difficult to temper. A cone-belt ought to be of the best material and have no butts or thick parts. These make the ends bob, and often deceive us regarding their tightness.

CHAPTER XI.

DIFFICULTIES PRACTICALLY OVERCOME.

THE TWIST IN ROVING—GOOD RULES— THE BEST METHODS OF SIZING SLIVER—SIZING THE FINE DRAWING—PRACTICAL SUGGESTIONS—HANK-TABLE—INFLUENCE OF TEMPERATURE ON DRAWING—A CAUSE OF UNEVEN NUMBERS—HOW TO TAKE CARE OF THE FRAMES—THE PREVENTION OF WASTE—A RECEIPT FOR GOOD ROLLER VARNISH.

The Twist in Roving.—Twist in roving not only affects the spinning as relates to quantity and quality, but in the card-room, if it is not soft enough to draw well on intermediate and fine speeders, simular results are experienced, and the thoroughly practical carder always knows whether the proper twist is on the rove or not, by giving his attention to these frames. Theory cannot be depended on, in regulating the twist on roving. Experience in preparing different grades of stock is absolutely necessary in order that sound judgment may be used in applying to the roving, in every process, the twist that will assure the best results. Practical carders are well aware that any attempt to twist roving by rule is a very perilous operation, and the effects

of such efforts are often absurd. Different causes produce different effects. The cotton fibre is liable to variations in several ways, and according to these variations, the degree of twist on the roving must vary also. Sudden atmospheric changes which affect the cotton while passing through the several machines must be carefully studied, and the suitable twist-gear kept ready. The let-off gear is also effective in keeping the roving good during changes of the weather. Still, this does not prevent us from starting with the correct rule by which to get twist, and afterwards satisfying ourselves as to its reliability. Strength enough to pull the bobbin round in the creel without weakening the rove in any way, is as good a rule as any.

The English standard twist per inch for one hank roving is 1.20 while the American is $\frac{8}{100}$ more, and the rule to find the requisite twist for any hank-roving is this :

RULE FOR TWIST OF ROVING.

Take the square root of the hank-roving desired and multiply by the standard twist per inch on one hank-roving, which will give you the necessary twist per inch.

ANOTHER RULE.

A very safe rule by which to calculate the twist for roving, and which applies to slubbers

and intermediates perhaps more than to fine speeders, on account of its simplicity, is to take the decimal .85 for a standard, and multiply by the hank-roving. The product will be the twist per inch required for said hank.

These rules, combined with experience and practical common sense, will answer every purpose for preparing roving for the spinning. They must be used only as guides to inform the carder that he is pretty near to the right twist, after which he must arrange it with reference to the requirements of the staple. If the cotton in use has a long, strong fibre, it will not need so much twisting as cotton with a medium fibre; while cotton with a very short fibre must have more twist than the medium. The object is to have the roving soft, so that it will draw well in the following process, and at the same time strong enough to stand the strain which will be given to it in the creels.

In some places the cotton used varies much in condition and length of fibre from time to time, which is very annoying, and prevents the carder from getting his rove forward in the state he desires, especially with the proper twist. The reason for this is that the shorter portion runs in with the longer and cannot be detected in time to make the desired change.

The best Methods of Sizing. — Every

card-room must have some positive method by which to determine whether the sizes are too heavy or too light. If a mill is intended to weave 40-inch goods to weigh 3½ yards per pound, a variation of ten per cent. in this weight makes trouble at once with the financial department of the concern, because the cloth is too light or too heavy; and the blame generally falls upon the carder. Now, when a carder takes one yard of sliver from the railway-head or drawing frame, but most generally from the former, and weighs it to ascertain whether the machine is regulating at the standard weight or not, and makes changes on the test which must go forward in the different processes until it reaches thread or cloth, he is working on a very poor basis. The sizing of the sliver ought to lead to a positive result and the length measured should, to accomplish this with any degree of certainty, be not less than twelve yards. But this is somewhat tedious in places where the yard is laid off on a board. We will, therefore, give a description of a little arrangement by which the carder is enabled to measure the sliver or roving with remarkable exactitude to any desired length.

It consists of a pulley, the circumference of which is either ¼ or ½ of one yard, with an upper roll, to keep the drawing or roving in contact with the measuring surface. The index-gear

is subdivided, one circle being revolutions, and the other yards. Some of these little machines have an attachment outside of the large pulley, by which the number of twists per inch in the roving can be readily shown. This is a very complete and necessary appliance for the card-room and together with an accurate instrument to weigh on, forms an apparatus that is efficient for measuring and weighing, and from which good results will be obtained.

In the cotton mills in England much more consideration is given to the methods for keeping the numbers correct, than we find at home. When the writer worked there, in 1856, there was a little machine used for sizing roving, the like of which he has not seen since. It was very artistically made with beam and scales directly in front of the pulley. When the bobbins were set on the creel, the ends, after passing over the pulley, were delivered into the scale and the operation of turning continued until the beam was exactly balanced. The size was taken. There was nothing more to do but to look at the indexes, which were on two gears, one of which contained 99 teeth and the other 100, and both pitched into the same worm. The 99 gear indexed the hanks and the 100 teeth gear the decimal parts of one hank. This was at that time considered a very ingenious and perfect sizing

apparatus, and no doubt is in operation in many places yet.

Sizing the Fine Drawing.—In fine factories where the carder must be still more careful with the numbers, an excellent plan is to size the fine drawing head at least three times a day. For this purpose there are many devices which will measure with great accuracy 30 yards of sliver. The same plan ought to be extended to all the mills; it would be of great advantage and would pay well for the trouble.

Practical Suggestions.—There is really no better way by which to keep correct sizes, than with a machine like one of those described, which will measure with certainty 30 yards. Size the roving frequently, that is to say slubber, inter-mediate and finishing, of each section; for all the room may not be running on the same hank. Some prepare two or three, and even more, differ-ent sizes of roving in the one room. When we say each section, we mean the slubbing, intermed-iate and finishing, of every system on which dif-ferent hank-roving is being made. The carder can mark off on his roving table, the hank, or weight in grains, the 30 yards from each of the frames ought to weigh, and note the correct weights each time regularly down. These will tell at all times the variations and will be of great benefit for reference.

Besides, there is nothing easier to calculate the hank by than 30 yards. Multiply 30 by 8⅓, which equals 250 which being divided by the weight in grains, the quotient is the hank. Surely this is simple enough; 250 always the "standard" number to be divided by the weight in grains. The utility of such a method of keeping numbers in our climate will be seen at a glance. It enables the carder to put on or take a tooth off of any the machines and thereby to prevent irregularities from getting to the spinning. If this system were thoroughly carried out, there would not be one-tenth of the poor spinning there is, because we depend too much on the automatic evener of the railway head. And all of us know that it does not or never was guaranteed to keep numbers even. We append a hank-table for 30 yards of roving:

HANKS FOR THIRTY YARDS.

Nos.	Grains.	Nos.	Grains.	Nos.	Grains.	Nos.	Grains.
.1	2500.	2.5	100.	4.9	51.02	7.3	34.25
.2	1250.	2.6	96.15	5.	50.	7.4	33.79
.3	833.3	2.7	92.06	5.1	49.02	7.5	33.33
.4	625.	2.8	89.29	5.2	48.08	7.6	32.90
.5	500.	2.9	86.21	5.3	47.17	7.7	32.47
.6	416.6	3.	83.33	5.4	46.3	7.8	32.05
.7	357.14	3.1	80.65	5.5	45.45	7.9	31.67
.8	312.5	3.2	78.12	5.6	44.64	8.	31.25

Nos.	Grains.	Nos.	Grains.	Nos.	Grains.	Nos.	Grains.
.9	277.7	3.3	75.82	5.7	43.86	8.2	30.49
1.	250.	3.4	73.53	5.8	43.10	8.3	30.12
1.1	227.27	3.5	71.43	5.9	42.37	8.4	29.76
1.2	208.3'	3.6	69.44	6.	41.66'	8.5	29.40
1.3	192.3	3.7	67.57	6.1	40.98	8.6	29.07
1.4	178.57	3.8	65.8	6.2	40.32	8.8	28.40
1.5	166.6'	3.9	64.10	6.3	39.70	8.9	28.09
1.6	156.25	4.	62.5	6.4	39.06	9.	27.77
1.7	147.	4.1	60.97	6.5	38.46	9.2	27.17
1.8	138.9	4.2	59.52	6.6	37.88	9.4	26.59
1.9	131.58	4.3	58.15	6.7	37.31	9.5	26.31
2.	125.	4.4	56.81	6.8	36.76	9.6	26.04
2.1	119.05	4.5	55.55	6.9	36.23	9.7	25.77
2.2	113.63	4.6	54.35	7.	35.72	9.8	25.51
2.3	108.7	4.7	53.19	7.1	36.21	9.9	25.25
2.4	104.16	4.8	52.08	7.2	34.72	10.	25.

The Influence of Temperature on Drawing.

—Tests and experiments carefully taken with a desire to ascertain the cause or causes of the work at one time grading light and at another heavy and strong, have shown some important results in regard to the effect the various conditions of humidity and temperature have upon the sliver. In our climate atmospheric changes are frequent. The influence of these is often felt, and causes a little variation betimes; yet by the use of atomizers and other artificial means, now well developed, we can control the atmosphere within the rooms so as partially to

overcome the excess of moisture on the one hand and the action of electricity on the other. In England or Scotland may be seen how well the work runs, surrounded by an atmosphere peculiarly adapted for spinning ; yet in those factories where the laws of nature are more potent than atomizers, there are spells of good and bad spinning, and sometimes very uneven numbers.

One of these tests was made with Middling New Orleans Cotton. It was a very damp, warm day, with 85 per cent. of moisture—just the kind of weather when cotton draws hard, because the fibres adhere more closely and the drawing between the rolls is not so regular as it ought to be. With a good magnifying glass we could easily discern that the drawing was not uniform, and although the rollers were in good form, and set, the fleece was cloudy. From this we were convinced there was too much moisture in the room, and that the cotton was absorbing more than was necessary for good work. The heat, combined with the excessive moisture, made one think that a fan, with some kind of an atomizer, would do much good.

On another occasion, when the air contained but 58 per cent. of moisture, and the electricity as severe in its action upon the cotton, the fibres were found standing off from the bulk of the sliver. This kind of temperature is probably the

worst of any with which the carder has to contend. Air containing an excess of moisture extends over but a few weeks, while the difficulties attending the dry electric atmosphere are very extended. Now, what practical means should carders have at hand to prevent the numbers from altering through these atmospheric changes? In the first place, they ought to know the condition of the atmosphere, both dry and wet. To find this out, they must have wet and dry bulb thermometers, and note them faithfully. These ought to be hung in the centre of the room, open to atmospheric changes. By the use of these instruments the carder will get acquainted with the best temperature for keeping numbers, so that the hank roving, counts spun and weight of cloth will always approximate very close to the standard. Without this aid, no carder can tell the variations of the atmosphere, unless these are extreme. The practical rule is, if the weather is at an even temperature, say of 75, with a relative humidity of 60 to 65, these are the best conditions for making good work in the cardroom. Keep the work to the standard on the railway head. But when you find you are surrounded with an atmosphere exceedingly dry, with between 35 and 40 relative humidity, keep the work at the railway head a grain or two heavy. And when a damp spell comes on and

the humidity runs up, you will be safe in letting the weight at the railway head run a grain or two under the standard. Cotton acted on by the electricity will not close together, and consequently will cause more friction in the trumpet, so that less fibre will pass through; and if kept to the standard weight will shade light, while on a damp day the fibre lies closer together and passes through the regulator with less friction, and permits a gain in the weight.

Another cause of Uneven Numbers.—The unsteadiness of the numbers is a subject which embraces the whole science of cotton spinning, and is a matter of such importance to all concerned, that no effort should be spared to maintain uniformity of weight and strength in the yarn. There are more disturbing elements by which the numbers are varied than those of temperature. In practice, the greatest unevenness has invariably been found when new cotton is being brought forward. It takes a number of days to get the new stock in and clear out the old, and until such time the carder is in a dilemma and can do nothing more than guess to which side the new stock will incline. The length of time he remains in this state of uncertainty depends upon how much of the cotton is stored by in laps, cans, or on bobbins. Of course, if he is methodical he will get rid of all he can, and arrive

at a definite conclusion as soon as possible. But this is not all. The rollers may be required to be adjusted to the new staple, and in the meantime some of it has got mixed in with the old, and the rollers cannot be touched, nor indeed can the truth be discovered, until the old is all out. This will be about the time it begins to tell in the spinning, and if it does not chance to come right, the work is bad, the roving is cut, the numbers are uneven, and in fact everything is in a disturbed state, until the rollers, are got right, the sizes steadied down, and the spinning creels filled anew.

How to take Care of the Frames.—To work to the best advantage is the duty of every carder. In order to do this he must have his frames leveled up every time they require it. No overseer who works around a speeder can fail soon to discover whether it is off the level or not. The frames should be thoroughly cleaned, and the steel rollers scoured, the joints disconnected and lubricated, and the stands adjusted once a quarter. When the rolls are dried well and put back in place a little piece of tallow should be put on each bearing. It ought to be seen to, at this time that the cap-bars, especially these in which the front roller stand, are not worn so that the covered rollers will not stand parallel with the flutes on the steel rolls. The covered rollers ought

to be all tried, to make sure that the leather is tight on them. The traverse-guide should be tested with the hand, while the rollers are out, to make sure that it travels far enough. The rails ought to be cleaned and tallowed as often as the rolls, and the spindle and bobbin-gears examined to see that they are properly pitched. The steps should be oiled once a week. The compound motion is so sensitive that it must be kept running free, because its regularity secures a more even drag on the roving, and produces more quantity and a better quality.

Look out for undue friction on the rail slides, and ballance weight pulleys. Be careful that the rack is well oiled and runs easy. Make your bobbins as large as you can, and see that the builder is not running too wide, and leaving a space between the winds on the bobbin. In this case your frame will be hard to temper, and you will not get so much on the bobbin. There is so much time spent in doffing that it pays to look after the small things.

To train the help against waste.—The carder is responsible for the establishing of a fixed system of procedure, the carrying out of which will ensure the greatest chance to produce the most and the best, with the least possible waste. In the best regulated rooms so much pains are taken in instructing the help that very lit-

tle of the work is allowed to go back in waste. This is simply and easily accomplished by the practical carder who devotes his attention principally to one thing until he is satisfied that his labor is sufficiently appreciated, and the reason made apparent to the worker. He must not be discouraged at the result of the first effort to economize, but must persevere, fully realizing the difficulties to be surmounted. He must make his help interested by reasoning with and illustrating to them the necessity of entering into any project by which real good can be done and through which their services shall be the more appreciated. Carders must, to be successful, train their help well concerning the making of waste. This should be kept down by every means. There are several sorts of waste in the preparation department which can, and ought to be avoided, and that object is materially assisted by the use of a good varnish.

A receipt for a good Roller Varnish.—6 ozs. of cooper's gelatine, 1 oz. of common glue, 1 oz. gum arabic, 4 ozs. alcohol, 1 quart water. Soak the glue and gelatine separately in vinegar over night and gum arabic in water: boil 20 minutes, then add 6 ozs. of vermilion dry. When cold it will be about the consistency of cheese. When wanted for use, heat to 150 degrees, spread on with a brush. The rolls are ready for use in one hour.

CHAPTER XII.

CARD-ROOM CALCULATIONS.

TO FIND THE DRAFT OF ANY MACHINE—DRAG BETWEEN DOFFER AND CALENDER ROLLS—DRAFT OF RAILWAY HEAD—OTHER MISCELLANEOUS RULES FOR MAKING CALCULATIONS.

To Find the Draft of any Machine.— Multiply the revolutions per minute of the back roller by its diameter for a divisor, and for a dividend multiply the revolutions, per minute, of the front roller by its diameter.

EXAMPLE 1.

The feed rollers of a card which is $1\frac{1}{8}$ inches in diameter makes $2\frac{1}{4}$ revolutions per minute, and the delivering roller, which is $2\frac{1}{2}$ inches in diameter, makes 61 revolutions per minute; required the drafts of the card.

$$\frac{25.0\times61}{2.25\times1.125}=60.24.$$

EXAMPLE 2.

The feed rollers of a card which is $2\frac{1}{2}$ inches in diameter and makes 2.85 revolutions per min-

ute, and the doffer 30 inches in diameter 12.35 revolutions, what is the draft from feed to doffer?

$$\frac{30 \times 12.35}{2.50 \times 2.85} = 52.$$

Another Rule.—Count the number of turns of the front roller for one of the back, this multiplied by the diameter of the front roller and divided by the diameter of the back will give the drafts as before.

EXAMPLE.

The turns of the front rollers for one of the back are $6\frac{1}{2}$, the diameter of the front roller is $1\frac{1}{8}$ and the diameter of the back $\frac{7}{8}$, required the draft.

$$\frac{9 \times 6.50}{7} = 8.36.$$

In taking the Draft of a Carding Engine call the Feed-Roller Gear the First Driver.
—Multipy all the drivers and the diameter of the feed roller together for a divisor, and all the drivers and diameter of the doffer or delivering roller for a dividend ; the quotient will be the draft.

EXAMPLE.

The feed roller gear of a roller-card contains 120 teeth and drives a pinion of 21 teeth on end of extension shaft, on the other end of which

128

there is a 40 gear driving a 30 pinion on end of doffer, the diameter of the feed roller is 2 inches, and that of doffer 23 inches. It is required to find the draft of this engine doffer.

$$\frac{120\times40\times23}{21\times30\times 2}=87.62$$

On this card there is a draw box, the back roller of which is $1\frac{2}{8}$ in diameter, and the front roller $1\frac{4}{8}$ in diameter. The back roller pinion of 26 teeth is driven by a 32 and the first roller pinion of 21 teeth driven by a 26. What is the total draft

$$\frac{120\times40\times23\times26\times36\times14}{21\times30\times 2\times32\times21\times12}=142.38.$$

EXAMPLE 2.

A front feed card feed rol-

ler gear has	73 teeth	⎤
Stud bevel gear	50 "	⎥ drivers.
Side shaft bevel gear	35 "	⎥
Gear on doffer pulley	26 "	⎦
Diameter of calender roll	$3\frac{7}{8}$ inches	
Gear on calender roll	24 teeth	⎤
Bevel gear on doffer pully	37 "	⎥ drivers.
Side shaft bevel gear	12 "	⎥
Stud gear	11 "	⎦
Diameter of feed roll	$1\frac{3}{8}$ inches	

$$\frac{73\times50\times35\times26\times3\frac{7}{8}}{24\times37\times12\times11\times1\frac{3}{8}}=79.85.$$

EXAMPLE 3.

Common back feed card first driver					138
				Driving a pinion	13
"	"	"	"	second driver	67
				Driving a pinion	16
"	"	"	"	third driver	27
				Driving a pinion	30
"	"	"	"	fourth driver	18
				Driving a pinion	37
			Diameter of condensing role		3⅞
		"	'of feeding role		1⅜

$$\frac{138 \times 67 \times 27 \times 18 \times 31}{13 \times 16 \times 30 \times 37 \times 11} = 54.81.$$

To Change the Carding from one Weight to Another.

—If less weight is required say, as the greater weight is to the lesser so is the present gear to the required gear, but if more weight be required say, as the lesser weight is to the greater so is the present gear to the required gear.

What feed pinion will be required to change the weight of the carding from 60 grains per yard to 48 grains, the present feed pinion bung having 15 teeth?

As 60 : 48 : : 15 : 12 the pinion required. Suppose that you want to change from 48 grains of

the yard to 60 grains say: As 48 : 60 :: 12 : 15 the change gear required. This rule is applicable to drafts in the same manner.

To Prove Whether there is any Drag between the Doffer and the Calender Rolls.
—Multiply the calender roll gear by the diameter of the doffer for a divisor, and for a dividend find the product of the doffer gear and the diameter of the calender roll. Whatever is more than one in the quotient will be the drag.

EXAMPLE.

The doffer gear is 128 and the diameter of the calender roll 3⅜ and the calendar roll gear is 32 and diameter of doffer 13⅜ to find the drag.

$$\frac{128 \times 27}{32 \times 107} = 1.002 - \frac{2}{1000}\text{ths the drag.}$$

To find the take up between the back roller of a railway head and the surface speed of the traveling railway belt.—Find the product of the revolutions per minute of the driving shaft, the diameter of driving pulleys and the teeth in driving gears, and divide by the product of the diameter of driven pulleys, and teeth in driven gears for a divisor.

Then find the product of the revolutions of driving shaft and the number of teeth in driving gears, and diameter of drum and belt. And

divide by the product of the number of teeth in the driven gears for a dividend and the quotient will be the take-up minus one.

Speed of pulley shaft 180 per minute on which is first driven 17 teeth driving 43. Second driver 18 driving 50. Third driver 21 driving 59. Diameter of drum and belt 6⅛ inches.

$$\frac{180\times17\times18\times21\times6\frac{1}{8}}{43\times50\times59}=\frac{\text{Inches.}}{55.85}\text{ speed of railway belt.}$$

Speed of pulley shaft 180, first driver is 5¾ inches in diameter driving another pulley 6¼ inches in diameter and on end of short shaft is second driver 24 teeth driving a 72 on end of back roller the diameter of which is 1⅛ inches.

$$\frac{180\times5.75\times24\times1.375}{72\times6.25}=62.09\text{ speed of back roll.}$$

$$\frac{62.09}{55.85}=1.11\frac{\text{Inches.}}{100}\frac{11}{100}\text{ is therefore the take-up.}$$

Fluted roller gear, 25; condensing roller gear, 43; diameter of fluted roller, 1½ inches; diameter of condensing roller, 2½ inches, what is the drag or take-up?

$$\frac{43\times1.50}{25\times2.50}=1.016\text{ take-up }\frac{16}{1000}\text{ths.}$$

To find the draft of the railway head at any part of the cones.—Find the product of

the revolutions per minute of the driving cone shaft, the diameter of the driving cone, and the driving gear of the front speed, and divide by the product of the diameter of the driven cone and the driven gears of the front speed for a dividend. Then find the product of the revolutions per minute of the driving shaft, the diameter of the driving pulley, and the driving gears of the back speed. Divide by the diameter of the driven pulley and the driven gears for a divisor. Then multiply the quotient of the back speed by the diameter of the back roll for a divisor, and the quotient of the front speed by the diameter of the front roller for a dividend.

EXAMPLE.

The revolutions per minute of the cone shaft 180, diameter of driving cone 7 inches, diameter of driven cone 7 inches, driving gear on driven cone shaft 28 teeth, and driven gear on front roller 24.

$$\frac{180 \times 7 \times 28}{7 \times 24} = 2.10, \text{ speed of front roll.}$$

The revolutions per minute of shaft 180, diameter of driving pulley for back speed 5.75, diameter of driven pulley 6.25, driving gear 24, and driven gear 72.

$$\frac{180 \times 5.75 \times 24}{6.25 \times 72} = 55.2, \text{ speed of back roll.}$$

$$\frac{210 \times 1\frac{3}{8}*}{55.2 \times 1\frac{1}{8}\dagger} = 4.65,$$ draft of railway head to front roll, when the belt is at a 7-inch part of the cone.

To find the draft of drawing, beginning at front roll.

—The product of the drivens and the diameter of the front roller divided by the product of the drivers, and the diameter of the back roller will give the draft.

EXAMPLE.

Front roller pinion 20 driving first stud gear 48, on the hub of which is a pinion 36, driving second stud or crown gear 60, on the hub of which is the change pinion 34 driving back roller 40, the front roller 1⅜ inches in diameter and and the back roll 1 inch, to find the draft:

$$\frac{48 \times 60 \times 40 \times 11}{20 \times 36 \times 34 \times 8} = 6.47, \text{ draft.}$$

To find the speed the back roll ought to run to take up what the front roll produces.

—Multiply the speed of the front roll by its diameter by the time it works per day, and by the number of ends delivering at the same time, and divide by the number of ends up at the back of the next machine supplied by these deliveries, the time the machine works per day, and the diameter of the back roll.

---

* Diameter of front roll.

† Diameter of back roll.

At what speed must the back roller of a slubber revolve per minute, its diameter being ⅞ of an inch, and the number of ends up 80, so as to uptake what is delivered from the drawing, the condensing roller of which revolves 220 times per minute and the diameter 2½ inches, the stoppages on both machines being equal, and the number of ends delivering at drawing 2.

$$\frac{220 \times 2\frac{1}{2} \times 2}{60 \times \frac{7}{8}} = 20.95 \text{ turns.}$$

To find the draft of a combing machine.

—NOTE. The index wheel and the cam shaft go at one speed. The index wheel is on the cylinder shaft and driving the feed is with a pin on this shaft. The pinion on end of cam-shaft drives the delivery. The ratchet gear which drives the detaching shaft and front roller is also driven by the cam-shaft one turn of which makes one teeth of rachet.

The product of the turns of the detaching roller, for one of the ratchet gear and its diameter divided by the product of the turns of the feeding roller; for one of the ratchet gear and its diameter will be the draft.

In a combing machine the ratchet gear has 20 teeth and the wheel on end of ratchet shaft

138, pinion on detaching or front roller 18, and the diameter of said roller $\frac{7}{8}$ of an inch.

Notched gear driven by feed pin 5 teeth pinion on end of notched gear shaft driving feed roller 19, gear on feeding roller 38, diameter of feeding roller $\frac{3}{4}$ of an inch. Required the draft.

$$\frac{138}{18}\times\frac{7}{8}\div\frac{4\times19}{38}\times\frac{3}{4}=\frac{966}{144}\div\frac{228}{152}=4.47 \text{ draft.}$$

THE FOLLOWING RULES ARE FROM A BOOK BY JOSEPH CHEATHAM.

To find a twist wheel for a roving frame in changing from one number of hank to another.—Take the square root of the hanks roving required for a divisor, and for a dividend multiply the square root of the hanks roving you are making by the twist-wheel you have on.

EXAMPLE.

If a roving-frame is making a 2½-hank roving with a 36 twist-wheel, what would a 5-hank require?

2,23 : 1,58 : : 36 : 25 twist-wheel required.

To find a rack-wheel for a slubbing or roving frame in changing from one hank to another.—Take the square root of the hanks roving or slubbing you are making for a divisor, and for a dividend multiply the square root of

136

the hanks roving or slubbing required by the rack-wheel you have on.

EXAMPLE.

Suppose in making a 1½-hank slubbing or roving with a 22-rack wheel, what would a 2¼ hank require?

1,22 : 1,50 : : 22 : 27 rack-wheel required.

To find a change-wheel in changing from one hank roving to another.—Take the hanks roving required for a divisor, and for a dividend multiply the hanks roving you are making by the change-wheel you have on.

EXAMPLE.

Suppose a frame making a 3 hank roving with a 38 change-wheel, what wheel would you require to make a 5½-hank roving?

5,5 : 38 : : 3 : 20 change-wheel required.

To find a change-wheel to give a required hank slubbing from a given hank drawing.—Multiply the front-roller pinion, hank slubbing required, and diameter of back roller together for a divisor, then multiply the carrier-wheel, back-roller wheel, hanks drawing, and diameter of front roller together for a dividend.

EXAMPLE.

If the front-roller pinion of a slubbing frame contains 18 teeth, carrier wheel 72, back roller

wheel 44, hanks drawing ¼ hank, diameter of front roller 1 inch or ⅜ths, back roller ⅞ths, required a change pinion to produce a 1½-hank slubbing.

$$
\begin{array}{ccc}
18 & : & 72 \\
1,5 & & 44 \\
90 & & 288 \\
18 & & 288 \\
\hline
27,9 & & 3168 \\
7 & & 8 \\
\hline
189,0 & & 25344 \\
& & ,25 \\
\hline
& & 126720 \\
& & 50688 \\
\hline
\end{array}
$$

189,0)63360,0(33 pinion required.

NOTE.—If there are two ends put up at back of the slubbing frame multiply the divisior by 2.

To draw a required hanks roving from a given hanks slubbing is found in exactly the same manner.

To find a change-wheel for a roving frame in changing from one hank roving to another when the hank slubbing is altered.—Multiply the hanks slubbing to be

altered from by the hanks roving required for a divisor, and for a dividend multiply the hanks roving to be altered from by the hanks slubbing you are going to work, and that product by the change-wheel.

Suppose a roving frame was making a 2-hank roving with a 33 pinion, and a ¼-hank slubbing, what pinion would be required to produce a 3-hank roving from a ½-hank slubbing?

```
,25   :   ,50   :   33
 3    :    2
_____     _____

75        100
           33
          _____

          300
          300
          _____
```

75)3300(44 pinion required.

NOTE.—The same rule also applies to a slubbing frame.

To find the hanks roving when the slubbing is altered.—Take the slubbing you are working for a divisor, and for a dividend multiply the slubbing you are going to work by the roving you are making.

Suppose a ¼-hank slubbing produce a 2-hank roving, what will a ¾-hank slubbing produce?

,25 : ,75 : : 2 : 6 hanks roving.

To find the hanks slubbing when the roving is altered.

—Take the hanks roving you are making for a divisor, and for a dividend multiply the roving required by the hanks slubbing you are working.

Suppose a ¼-hank slubbing produce a 2-hank roving, what hank slubbing will be required to produce a 6-hank roving?

2 : ,25 : : 6 : ,75 or ¾-hanks slubbing.

To find the draft of slubbing or roving frames.

—Multiply the front-roller pinion, change pinion, and diameter of back-roller together for a divisor, and for a dividend multiply the carrier-wheel, back-roller wheel and diameter of front roller together. Reduce the diameter to 8ths of an inch.

Suppose the diameter of back roller be 1⅛ inch, front roller 1¼ inch, front pinion 22 teeth, change pinion 26 teeth, carrier wheel 78 teeth, back-roller wheel 36 teeth, required the draft.

```
26              78
22              36
___            ___
52             468
52             234
___           ____
572           2808
 9              10
____          _____
5148      )28080(5,45 draft
```

The hanks roving you are making divided by the hanks slubbing you are working will give you the draft.

Suppose the slubbing was ½-hank, the roving 3-hank, required the draft.

,50)3,00(6 draft.

The draft and hank slubbing given, to find the hanks roving.

The hank slubbing multiplied by the draft will give you the hank roving you are making.

Suppose a frame had a ½-hank slubbing put up at the back, and a 6 of a draft, what would be the hanks roving ?

$$\frac{,50}{6}$$

3,00 hank roving.

NOTE.—If 2 ends put up at the back, divide the quotient by 2.

To find the hanks slubbing.—The hanks roving you are working divided by the draft will give the hanks slubbing.

EXAMPLE.

Suppose the draft was 6, the hanks roving 3, required the hanks slubbing you are working.

6)3,00(,50 or ½ hank slubbing.

To find the length of yarn delivered from the rollers of a slubbing or roving frame in a given time.—Multiply the number of revolutions by the circumference of front roller.

EXAMPLE.

If the front roller of a frame makes 70 revolutions per minute, required the length of yarn delivered, supposing the roller is 1 inch diameter.

$$\frac{3,1416}{70}$$

219,9120 or nearly 220 inches.

THE END.

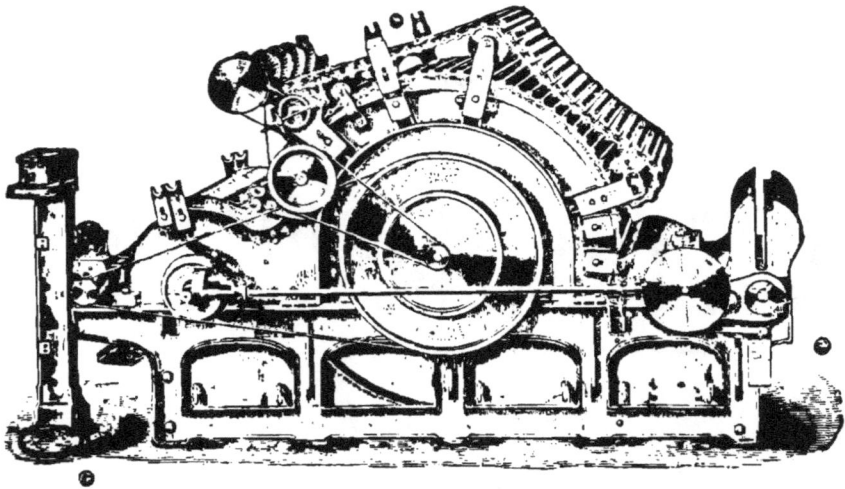

STEDMAN & FULLER MFG. CO.,

PROVIDENCE, R. I., U. S. A.

MANUFACTURERS OF

CARD CLOTHING

OF EVERY VARIETY,

Made of Leather, 6-ply Cotton, Woolen Cloth
or Vulcanized Rubber,

Tempered Steel or Common Wire.

N. B.—Tempered Steel Wire Cards Ground
if required.

PHILADELPHIA OFFICE:
236 Chestnut St.
R. HENRY, Agt.

WESTERN AGENTS:
Messrs. R. R. STREET & CO.,
188 and 190 Washington St.
CHICAGO.

Cotton Openers,
Cotton Lappers,

THREAD EXTRACTORS

—AND—

Waste Working Machinery.

WOOL WASHERS
and DRYERS.

Shoddy Pickers.

Kitson Machine Co.,

LOWELL, MASS.

FRANKLIN MACHINE CO.,

PROVIDENCE, R. I.

Cotton Mill Machinery

PARTICULAR ATTENTION PAID TO

SPINNING AND CARDING.

THE IMPROVED

FOSS & PEVEY

UNDERFLAT

COTTON CARD,

CYLINDER 36 x 36.

WILL CARD 150 LBS. PER 10 HOURS FOR

Nos. 12 AND 16 YARN.

JOHN M. PEVEY, Prop'r,

LOWELL, MASS.

See what the Author says, page 50.

D. F. ROBINSON,

MANUFACTURER OF

Card ✛ Clothing

OF EVERY DESCRIPTION

FOR

COTTON, WOOLEN AND FLAX MACHINERY

LAWRENCE, MASS.

—CORRESPONDENCE SOLICITED.—

HARDY MACHINE CO.,

MANUFACTURERS OF THE

Hardy Improved Traverse Emery Wheel

CARD GRINDERS,

—AND—

Card Grinding Machinery,

BIDDEFORD, MAINE.

✤ Fidelity ✤
Machine Works,

MANAYUNK,

PHILADEEPHIA, PA.,   *U. S. A.*

R. H. PATTON, Propr.

COTTON MACHINERY

☞ WRITE FOR CIRCULARS. ☜

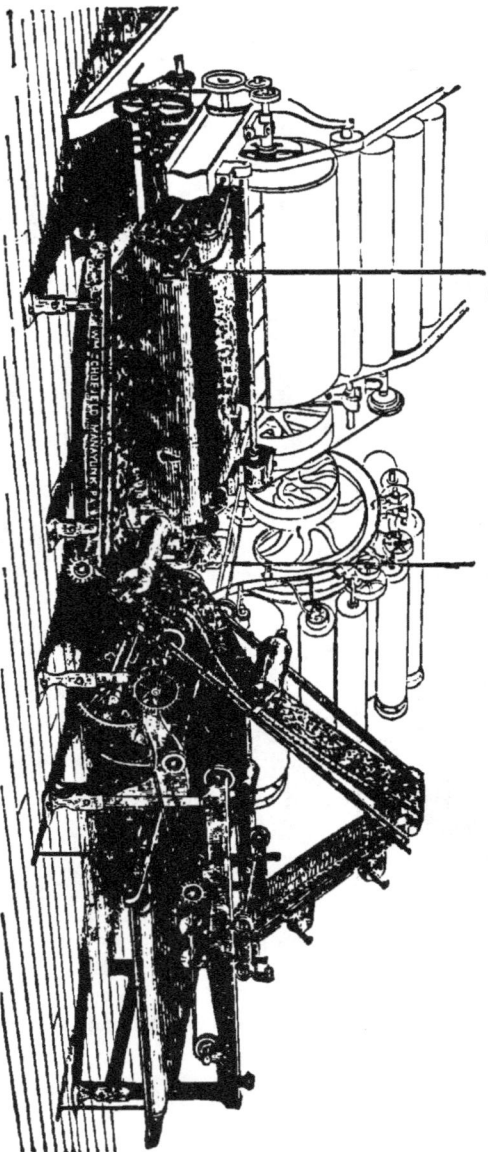

Arthur Young

Peace and Reform, Against War and Corruption
In Answer to a Pamphlet

ISBN/EAN: 9783743418615

Manufactured in Europe, USA, Canada, Australia, Japa

Cover: Foto ©Suzi / pixelio.de

Manufactured and distributed by brebook publishing software (www.brebook.com)

Arthur Young

Peace and Reform, Against War and Corruption

In Answer to a Pamphlet